Peace Inside

'This powerful book of hope and healing is both a guide and a moving account of prisoners' struggles and successes as they learn to meditate and to make sense of their life and prison experiences. It is written for prisoners, but it has much wider relevance too. It is about friendship, love and living truthfully. It draws on correspondence over many years between Prison Phoenix Trust staff and prisoners, showing how human beings can survive, and even flourish, in the most testing circumstances. This works when we are helped to reclaim the peace in ourselves, and to share it with others. Settie's *Peace Inside* is full of humanity. Read it!'

– *Alison Liebling, Professor of Criminology and*
Criminal Justice, University of Cambridge

'What a wonderful book. Clear, friendly, supportive, this is a super manual and introduction to meditation practice, not just for people inside but for all of us, inside and out. The writing from the prisoners is moving and luminous, and shows us all what meditation can do for a human being – the book is a teaching and a gift for us all.'

– *Henry Shukman, writer, poet and Director of*
Mountain Cloud Zen Center, USA

'Sam Settle's *Peace Inside* is a clear assistant along the path of yoga and meditation... Having myself spent a decade in prison, I found *Peace Inside* accessible, brilliant, and a welcome companion on the way to spiritual freedom.'

– *James Bishop, author of* A Way in the Wilderness *(Bloomsbury)*
and International Coordinator for Prison Outreach,
The World Community for Christian Meditation

'This book will change lives for the better for people who are locked up in places not readily associated with freedom, calm and personal insight. The gentle clarity throughout brings the seemingly impossible within reach and introduces a way of living that can bring a new light to life inside and beyond.'

– *Pete White, once a prisoner, now Chief Executive*
of Positive Prison? Positive Future

Peace Inside

A Prisoner's Guide to Meditation

Edited by Sam Settle

Foreword by Benjamin Zephaniah
Illustrated by Pollyanna Morgan

Jessica Kingsley *Publishers*
London and Philadelphia

First published in 2017
by Jessica Kingsley Publishers
73 Collier Street
London N1 9BE, UK
and
400 Market Street, Suite 400
Philadelphia, PA 19106, USA

www.jkp.com

Library of Congress Cataloging in Publication Data
Names: Settle, Sam, editor.
Title: Peace inside : a prisoner's guide to meditation / edited by Sam Settle.
Description: London ; Philadelphia : Jessica Kingsley Publishers, 2017.
Identifiers: LCCN 2016051843 | ISBN 9781785922350 (alk. paper)
Subjects: LCSH: Meditation. | Yoga. | Prisoners--Religious life. |
    Prisoners--Mental health.
Classification: LCC BL627 .P394 2017 | DDC 158.1/2086927--dc23 LC record
available at https://lccn.loc.gov/2016051843

British Library Cataloguing in Publication Data
A CIP catalogue record for this book is available from the British Library

ISBN 978 1 78592 235 0
eISBN 978 1 78450 528 8

Printed and bound in Great Britain

Dedicated to the memory of Pete N

Contents

The names of people writing from inside prison or who are now out of prison have been changed, except for Prison Phoenix Trust patrons Benjamin Zephaniah and Erwin James.

Foreword

Despite what some newspapers say, prison is no holiday camp. And despite the good intentions of many people charged with running prisons, you can wind up feeling less than human when you're inside. You know this, and I know this, and anyone who's been near a prison knows this. From the age of 14 I was in and out of institutions. It started with what was then called Approved School, then it was borstal, and then I ended up in prison for a while. I've written a lot in my life, but I haven't written much about my time in prison. The piece about my time in Winson Green prison in Birmingham, which you'll see in the letters section of this book, is an exception.

If you're finding it hard in prison – and very few people don't find it hard – meditation is something that will make a real difference. I have to say that I used to think meditation was something that men with long beards did in the mountains of India and China. Or that it was for monks who want to spend their time at peace with a candle rather than go shopping. Or hippies who just want to touch the everlasting and chill out, man. There's a little truth in all those stereotypes, but the fact is that all of us can benefit from meditation. Every human being on the planet understands that they better themselves when they take time to listen to themselves. I mocked meditators once, until I realised what it could do for me.

In this book, Sam, the Prison Phoenix Trust's (PPT) Director, explains meditation and how to meditate in a simple, straightforward way. What is equally important is that he's drawn together letters from people in prison who've written about their meditation, and replies to them from the PPT. These make great reading whether you're in prison or out.

Everyone has a natural intelligence, and I met some incredibly intelligent and creative people in prison. Meditation is a way of not just surviving, but also of thriving in prison, because it taps into that natural intelligence that we all have. Together with my martial arts, it is yoga and meditation that keep me healthy and sane. They support my poetry, music, writing, and all the other stuff I do on TV and radio. There was a time when I was struggling to survive and jostling on the streets, there was a time when I was caught and imprisoned, but there was also a time when I had all the money I needed, people loved me. I wasn't in prison and I was called successful, but I was still tired of life, and my spirit was sagging. It was meditation that pulled me through. I really got to know myself. You see, when I'm sitting still, focusing on my breathing, forgetting about myself and my little worries, plans and contracts, it's an honest expression of who I really am. Time alone each day helps me feel a little more human, and a little more connected to people and the world around me.

This book is encouragement for you to do that too.

Stay cool, wherever this finds you,

Benjamin Zephaniah

Introduction

There's a good chance you're reading this in a prison cell. Maybe you're in for a long time, or perhaps it's only a few months. Has the justice system let you down, or do you feel you deserve your sentence? Even if you are relatively content with your situation, there'll be times when you feel you can't stand even one more day of being where you are.

External conditions affect us and how we look at things. In prison, it's the amount of bang-up each week, how you get along with your cellmate, how safe and how much trust you feel, what work you've been assigned, and how your last phone call went. If things are going well, they can put you in a good mood, and you feel ready to meet anything that comes your way. But if where you are feels grim it can be very draining and you might want to just hole up and blot it all out. Isn't this how we are influenced by our surroundings and external conditions?

It's great to remember that there are people and organisations trying to make prison conditions and sentencing policy more humane. And it's fantastic that there are people fighting for change and educating others about why people end up in prison.

Perhaps you yourself are involved in this work while you're doing time. I take my hat off to you and anyone inside and outside of prison engaged in prison reform. It's uphill work but occasionally gleams of humanity break through, often from unexpected quarters.

This book is about a different kind of work. It isn't about changing the world around you to meet your needs (at least, not directly). Instead, it's an invitation to work with the most powerful thing affecting your moment-to-moment experience:

your own heart and mind.

It's about the tried-and-tested practices of meditation and yoga.

And it's about the fruit of those practices: living from a place of freedom in the truest sense of the word, right where you are, bars or no bars.

Unlike 'the system', which can seem rigid and unforgiving, our hearts and minds are flexible places we can dive into and work with at any moment. This very personal work offers huge potential for give and take, for change, for growth, for inspiration, for warmth, for love, for uncovering a part of ourselves that is true and deep. (And somehow, the *inner* work you do often starts to affect your external circumstances.)

As you can see from the letters in this book, so many people who have taken up this inner search have said that even though they are in prison, they have found this deep, true place in themselves, and that they are free. It's funny to have to go to prison to find freedom inside. Most people don't get any break from the madness and challenges of day-to-day living. Yet countless people testify that the practice of meditating while in prison and afterwards has led them to feel more at ease with who they are, and because of that they feel more connected and less separate from the world around them.

Three things motivate me in my work with the Prison Phoenix Trust. The first is you, living in the intense mental pressure cooker that is prison, and the inspiring ways that so many of you manage to find a sense of freedom. So a big part of this book is letters from prisoners, and people now out of prison. As you read them, I hope you'll see that inner freedom is possible, but that it doesn't always look like what you expect, and it isn't the same for everyone. The path of freedom is not always easy – it's often three steps forward and two steps back – but it's one worth walking. And as you read the letters, you'll see that despite it feeling like a slog at times, it brings deep and consoling satisfaction. Maybe it's a path you're already on. If so, respect and greetings.

The second thing that motivates me is the tried and tested practice of meditation and yoga. The letters from people who are committing themselves to these practices in a serious way are inspiring, especially when they feel their lives have begun to shift in a direction that they like and which feels a million times freer and more harmonious and more open to possibilities than before.

Interested? Later on, you'll find instructions on meditation, to help your mind and heart become clearer and quieter by concentrating on your breathing.

Although many of you tell us that doing yoga each day is a perfect complement to meditation, this book doesn't cover yoga. This is because we have free books and CDs to help you with a yoga practice. If you don't already have a yoga book or CD, write to the Prison Phoenix Trust and ask for them. The Trust also supports yoga and meditation classes in many UK and Irish prisons and in some special hospitals, immigration removal centres and bail hostels, because we know how valuable it is to have a teacher, and to practise in a group.

The third thing holding this book together is friendship. At its most basic level, friendship is the fundamental human act of reaching out past yourself to the other, going past apparent differences to find the common ground that is always here, connecting us to everyone and everything. This is both the starting point and the end of any path of change. You'll see that for many people in prison who have written over the years, finding ways of 'being there' for other people has helped them tap into something deeply human, bringing to life the connection and lack of separation that the practice is all about.

It seems to me that day-to-day living is a great challenge for all human beings, whether you have served time or not. There doesn't *appear* to be any magic solution that means you can avoid the messiness, pain and suffering of life. But I hope you'll see that one way of embracing *all* of life – its beauty, joy and laughter, as well as its problems, struggles and things that get on your nerves – is through the silence of meditation.

Whether you've been doing meditation for years or are brand new to it, know this: you are not alone. Throughout UK and Irish prisons, and in jails around the world, thousands of people delve deep into themselves by making the time to sit still in silent meditation each day. An even vaster number outside of prison put aside part of their day to do this too. And when you sit in meditation, know that you are not just with others but with the whole of creation, never separate. I hope this becomes more and more a wordless truth that seeps deeper into your bones with each breath you take.

Sam Settle, Director, Prison Phoenix Trust

PART I

Meditation

The first time I tried meditation, it was a disaster. This is what happened.

For years I'd heard about meditation and the way of living a trouble-free life that it seemed to offer. I'd always been interested in spirituality and going deep inside: I was raised as a Methodist, and so had learned how to pray. I'd read books on Zen and Eastern religions and Christian mysticism. I'd enjoyed the visualisations that my first yoga teacher led us through in each class. But I'd never really had a proper introduction to meditation.

It was more than just an intellectual interest for me, as life had started to throw up serious challenges when I was young and in my early twenties. My mum had died when I was 13 after a long illness. After that, divisions and discord in my family seemed to worsen. In my late teens, it slowly sank in that the alcoholism and physical abuse I'd been around as a child were having a bigger effect on me than I had previously realised. My mental health became fragile, leading to a brief stay in a secure hospital. At some point, I realised I'd had enough of reading and talking about meditation, and I just needed to do it.

I decided to take myself off for a weekend to a remote camping shelter I'd hiked past a few years earlier, along the Appalachian Trail. (This was in the United States, where I was born.) Armed with my sleeping bag, a bit of food and a water filter, I trekked deep into the woods of the Blue Ridge Mountains, until I reached the simple shelter, closed on three sides and open at the front, overlooking a gurgling creek. It was far from any roads, man-made noise, or other humans. It seemed perfect.

After unpacking the few things in my bag and exploring the creek and nearby woods for a while, I came back to the shelter to meditate. I had told myself that I would do nothing all weekend but meditate, prepare simple meals, use the toilet, and sleep. I remembered from yoga class how to sit cross-legged so I sat – with nothing underneath me to soften the hard wooden floor – and then closed my eyes, put my hands in some position I imagined to be special, and tried to clear my mind. I didn't know any way of doing this, so just tried to stop thinking.

At first, the novelty of being alone in the woods allowed me to keep going. But within 15 minutes, I was agitated. Despite wanting my mind to be clear, the thoughts were endless and uncontrollable. I had massive doubts about what I was doing, whether I was doing it right and whether I was cut out for it. Very strong in my mind was a desire to achieve some miraculous state of being. And yet, within a few minutes, my ankles, legs, groin and back all started to ache. Gradually, I got irritated with it all: the pain, the restlessness, the grand idea of achieving something special, and not actually knowing what the hell I was doing. All of these things made me so frustrated that I didn't last 30 minutes. Less than an hour after arriving, my things were packed and I started the long hike home, feeling foolish and ashamed, determined not to tell anyone what had happened. So much for my big weekend of teaching myself to meditate in the wild!

A couple of years later, though, there was a chance to give meditation another go, this time with more realistic expectations and the support of some kind people who had done it for years. They provided clear instructions and useful principles to bear in mind. As I started practising, I could talk with them about things that seemed hard. Gradually I came to appreciate the incredible depth and boundlessness of the human heart and mind, and how this depth seeps slowly – or floods quickly – into life, when the ordinary churning and ruminating of the mind is helped to become stiller and calmer. Since then, meditation has become a necessary and vital part of the day. Like cleaning my teeth.

If you are just setting out with meditation, you might find the frustrations I had initially. Don't worry. There's nothing to worry about. And anyway, you are probably far wiser than I was in my determination to crack open the mysteries of the universe, and of life and death, in one weekend!

CHAPTER 1

What Is Meditation?

Something inside me has reached the
place where the world is breathing.

Kabir, Indian poet, mystic and philosopher (1440–1518)

'For nearly nine months, I have been practising meditation. I still can't define it properly – exciting, torturing, empty, full, unbearable, unmissable. Perhaps it is for its mysterious simplicity that I can't help but do it every day… It's not about believing something or hoping for some kind of future happy resolution of my troubles. It's more about looking for real freedom through self-discovery.'

Antonio, HMP Lewes

What is meditation, and what do you do when you meditate?

Stop ten people on your wing or landing and ask them what meditation is, and you'll probably get ten different explanations. The kind of meditation explained in this book is focusing on the breath while sitting still. Just:

paying attention to your breathing.

When your attention wanders, bring it back to the breath. Even in the short span of five minutes, your attention may wander off dozens of times. A major part of meditation is learning how to return your attention – and return yourself – to what is happening right here and now. It's about returning to 'what is' again and again and again. And again. And again. And again and again.

It is frustrating at times, when your mind is all over the place while you are 'trying' to meditate. But that slow, difficult work of developing the mind's capacity to pay attention by bringing yourself back again and again (and again) to the breath *is what it's about*! This is the practice – and why it's called meditation *practice*.

Many of us have had things happen in our lives which leave terrible memories, nightmares or out-of-control thinking and anxiety. We might say to ourselves, 'That was then, this is now, and now it's safe.' But still, our feelings may run amok and make it hard to get on with other people and take control of life. By befriending the breath, making it your ally, you start to regain some control.

With time, persistence and ocean-loads of patience with yourself, life may start to feel a bit different. Ironically, by placing your attention on the breath, and not on your thoughts and feelings, you become more aware of your mind, and what's in your heart. When you don't pay attention, thoughts and feelings tend to come thick and fast, pushing you around, making you feel powerless and at the whim of something else, like a carrier bag blown around by the side of the motorway.

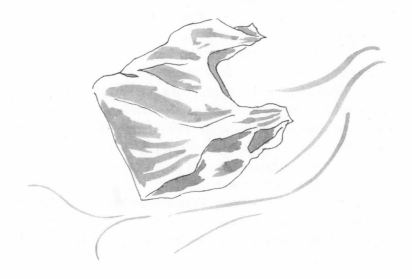

By taking time regularly to train the mind's attention in the breath, the power of the thoughts and feelings is lessened. It's quieter inside. It feels good, like when a pounding headache goes away. It feels good because a part of yourself that you really like – your deepest, truest nature – begins to come forward more and more as old thoughts and stories start to die down and the silence inside deepens.

What you are actually doing is simple: just keep attending to the breath. But because humans are so complex, driven by thoughts and feelings even when we aren't aware of it, meditation is also incredibly hard at times. But this practice is healing and far-reaching, because it shifts the way we relate to thoughts and feelings, and therefore it changes how we relate to our lives and the whole world.

What this style of meditation isn't

Of those ten people you stop in your prison, some of them would probably say that meditation is about having an out-of-body experience. Some might say it's about not thinking about anything. Or picturing yourself on a tropical beach or imagining walking through the woods or on top of a mountain. Some people would say it's lying down, chilling out, just letting your mind go. Others might think it's about repeating a particular word silently in your mind. Still others would say it's about thinking positive thoughts about yourself and others. Most would say it's about changing yourself for the better. Many would suggest it's about wiping out what's difficult. Some would say it's the same as getting stoned.

Thinking positive thoughts about yourself and others can be really useful; we've included some suggestions to help you do that at different places in the book. There's nothing wrong with chilling out and taking it easy either. And some types of meditation do encourage you to imagine yourself somewhere else. But none of that is what we're talking about here.

Meditation is about having an *in-body* experience. This means it's not about stopping thinking – as though we can switch off thinking at will! Instead it's about developing the capacity to be with oneself and one's thoughts and feelings, so that you start to relate to them in a different way. You are not trying to transport yourself in your mind to some other, beautiful, peaceful place, but in fact realising that right here where you are is okay – impossible as that may seem. In fact, it's the only place to be. Meditation respects and realises the true power of the mind by training it, with a posture of alertness, rather than simply letting everything go. It's about being with a part of yourself, and a part of reality too, that is deeper than any concepts or anything that you can imagine, by letting go of all words and ideas as you sink into the breath. It's about realising that this nameless part of yourself which comes forward from the depths of silence in meditation is completely connected to everything. It lacks nothing, and so doesn't need affirmation or improving. And above all, meditation is about being with what is difficult and messy outside and inside of oneself, and staying with it with patience, kindness and deep curiosity.

How is meditation related to religion?

Anyone can practise meditation, whether you follow a particular faith or not. This is possible because there isn't a set of beliefs or any dogma to sign up to. In fact, you just need to trust that you might feel better, and feel more in tune with the world. Actually, instead of piling up ideas or a set of beliefs, meditation is about letting go of ideas and assumptions and just resting in the breath.

This is by no means to say that you should stop thinking and feeling. On the contrary: meditation can make your thinking clearer and allow you to truly experience what you feel. As human beings we *need* to think and feel, and to plan and imagine and dream and remember. Is there anyone who doesn't want to try to make sense of the world? Strangely enough, all our mental activities we use each moment are a lot more interesting and fruitful when you let them rest a little bit each day while fully engaging with your breath, immersing yourself in the wordless inner silence that is always waiting.

Each of the world's religions has space for, and encourages, the inner silence of meditation practice. While institutionalised

23

religions may have pitfalls and dark sides, the teachings of the world's religions have been useful, indeed life-saving, to a vast number of people. Many people in prison say that their faith has become stronger as a result of taking up meditation and yoga. Others experience a sense of freedom through meditation and stretching the body, but don't need any religious framework to explain it. (You'll see a range of perspectives on faith and spirituality in the letters later in the book.)

I've always been sceptical of religion since I was made to go to church as a child. Looking back, I've never seen myself as 'religious', even when I ordained as a Buddhist monk in my twenties and lived for five years in a monastery in Thailand. But I've always been interested in how people from different traditions transform themselves – and how I might be able to do it myself too.

While I was in the Thai monastery, a small group of Catholic nuns from the Philippines came to live nearby, to study and practise meditation with us for a few months. They hoped that by studying the teachings of the monk who had founded our monastery and by living close to nature as we did, their own faith would be deepened and enriched: they were aiming to be better Christians.

After they finished their time with us, I had a chance to visit the nuns where they had gone to live a few provinces away. They had chosen to live alongside refugees who had fled fighting in neighbouring Burma. Unsupported by the Thai or Burmese governments, uncertain of their legal status in Thailand, afraid of returning to their homeland, the refugees were prone to all the overwhelming anxieties and troubles that beset people in refugee camps.

The nuns, who dressed much of the time in their Christian habit, had a small chapel where they worshipped mostly alone, faithful to their prayers and their daily services. At the same time, they had begun working with the refugees to help them revive the refugees' own traditions and rituals, which they'd lost sight of as their lives had been turned upside down by war, flight, homelessness and fear. The refugees' mix of Buddhism and animism[1] had supported them for generations and the nuns knew that it was the refugees' own faith, not Catholicism, that held the most hope for helping them with their uncertain future. The respect the nuns had for the religion and the culture of others, combined with a commitment to their own tradition, impressed me deeply.

If you find your own faith strengthened by meditation and yoga, great! If your path of inner discovery doesn't carry a name – or fit into any box – that's great too.

By the way, although I spent those early years as a Buddhist monk, this is not a Buddhist book. It is an invitation to silence. Meditation can benefit anyone of any faith, or none at all. Among the staff and volunteers at the Prison Phoenix Trust are Anglicans and Catholics, Quakers, Buddhists, Atheists, a Sufi, and Zen practitioners. We are lucky to count Christian priests, Jewish rabbis and Muslim imams among those who champion our work. It is in prison chaplaincies – as well as among gym staff and on drug rehab wings – that we find great support for our weekly yoga and meditation classes. All of these people, with different faiths and no faith at all, recommend tasting for yourself the fruit of silent, breath-based meditation.

---

1   Animism – the worldview that non-human entities such as animals, trees and objects have a spiritual essence.

CHAPTER 2

How to Meditate

Preparing your body

Certain messages from society say that human beings are just brains at the top of a stick, a head attached to the rest of the body, without the mental and physical selves affecting each other very much. In fact, as you know from your own experience, the condition of your body affects how you feel all the time, and it affects the 'tone' of your mind too. How you think and feel, how you see the world, what your ideas about yourself are – these in turn profoundly affect your physical well-being. The practices of yoga and meditation are rooted in this connectedness, so they work with the *whole* being: mental, physical, emotional and spiritual.

ABOUT THE WORDS 'YOGA' AND 'MEDITATION'
The practice of yoga includes not only postures and movements, but also sitting still, focusing the mind. You could say that yoga *includes* meditation. Not everyone teaching or practising yoga would agree: the world of yoga

is wonderfully diverse. I've benefited from the kindness and experience of teachers from many different schools. Some schools don't emphasise sitting still and training the mind in meditation and prefer to focus on postures, philosophy, or another element. Others would say that the postures and movements are a kind of meditation-in-motion and that seated meditation is too advanced for beginners. So there is a popular understanding of yoga as merely postures, and meditation as a vast array of different activities you can do with your mind. To keep it simple, I'll mean postures and movements when I say 'yoga' (although yoga has strong roots in seated meditation), and I'll mean the activity of sitting upright and alert, training the mind by focusing on the breath, when I say 'meditation'.

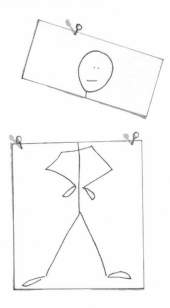

With this in mind, it's easy to see that if your body is relaxed, it's a lot easier to sit still and focus in meditation. Your body might be tense from gym work or doing sit-ups and push-ups in your cell. It might ache from lying on your bed all day. It might be stiff because of your work, whether that's something sedentary such

27

as making up breakfast packs or something more active such as planting out annual flowers with the grounds crew. Or perhaps you've just never learned how to help your body relax. It can be really hard to sit still in meditation, even for five minutes if your body is tense. Yoga is fantastic – almost magical! – because it helps you feel more at ease in your body, even if you feel it has let you down or you don't like it very much. This is why we recommend it, and why so many people in prison want to do it.

> 'I'm free for the first time in my life. This cell door doesn't mean squat to me, and that is the purpose of this letter, because you told me 18 months ago I could become free through meditation and yoga. I thought you were all obviously hippies with too much time on your hands. Lucky for me, I was bored enough to give it a shot.'
>
> *Liam, HMP Wandsworth*

If you haven't tried yoga before, don't knock it until you've had a go. I don't know of anything quite like it. It's simple, adaptable to suit the needs of each person – including those in wheelchairs – requires almost no equipment, costs nothing, works on all the body's systems, and can be highly dynamic and aerobic, or gentle and slow. It restores a sense of ease and contentment to the body, mind and emotions. Almost everyone says that they sleep better than they have in years on the night after their first go. Finally, like meditation, when you do it with complete focus on the breath, it helps free you from the crazy 'octopus of the mind', as one friend inside called his runaway thoughts and feelings, which cause difficulties for all human beings, inside or out of prison.

This book mentions yoga a lot, but doesn't go into detail. This is because we have free books for people in prison on yoga that explain what to do.

Creating a good space

Before you sit down to meditate, take a minute or two to clean and tidy the space you are in. Give it a sweep. Put any books, clothes and other things where they belong. Empty your ashtray if you have one. Some people light a candle and incense to give a nice atmosphere, to remind them of their inner light or the light which upholds the world. That's a nice thing to do, but by no means necessary. But perhaps there's a ledge, windowsill or a clear surface where you can put some things from the natural world – a flower, even if it's a paper flower you've made; or a stone, or piece of moss. Or an object that means something to you. The simpler the better.

(If you share a cell with someone who you think is going to find what you are doing weird, be respectful as you tidy, and take a look at the section later in this chapter: 'When to do it and for how long'.)

By tidying your space, you are making a clean, ordered environment for yourself which can support you as you meditate or practise yoga. It doesn't matter if you can hear (and smell) the rest of the prison. You aren't trying to build a cocoon for yourself, away forever from the chaos of life. You are just making room for peace in a small corner of your life, which you can appreciate and begin to like.

Inviting peace and clarity into your cell by cleaning your space is symbolic of an inward activity in your heart and mind. You are starting to take some control of your circumstances, rather than always letting them control you. When you clear away clutter, you create space for something new to come forward.

Thirty spokes share the wheel's hub; it is the centre hole that makes it useful.

Shape clay into a vessel; it is the space within that makes it useful.

Cut doors and windows for a room; it is the holes which make it useful.

Therefore profit comes from what is there; usefulness from what is not there.

from the Tao Te Ching, a Chinese philosophical text from the 4th century BC

When you find some small object that means something, especially if it reflects the beauty of the natural world, you can be reminded of your own beauty, your right to be here in the universe, and your own undoubted sacredness. These inherent qualities are here within you all the time, and can be most easily seen when the mind and heart are still and clear.

Everybody who begins to practise meditation finds it affects them in surprising ways. I liked a story that Brenda, a yoga teacher in Northern Ireland, told me. She said that after meditating every morning for 25 minutes for a month as part of her training to teach in prison, she got up one day after meditation and realised her kitchen needed painting. She hadn't noticed it before, and despite her busy life, she found time over the next week to give the kitchen a fresh coat of paint. She wasn't driven by a need to control external things, nor was she distracting herself from looking at something important inside. Instead it was a spontaneous response to what needed doing right around her. So prepare your space for sitting, and don't be surprised if your sitting tidies up your life in unexpected ways.

Sitting comfortably: how to arrange your body for meditation

Once you've invested a little bit of yourself in setting up your meditation area, it's time to sit down and arrange your body in the right position. It might seem crazy to recommend how to sit – surely it's just something we do naturally. But there are ways of sitting which make meditation a lot easier. As you know, your body and mind are not separate, so getting a good posture for meditation which you can sustain without strain is important. Spend as much time as you need to find a good sitting position using the pictures on these next pages. The main thing is to be comfortable, stable and upright.

If you aren't relatively comfortable, you'll probably spend your time just longing and hoping for the meditation practice to be over! You need to be physically stable, so you don't fall over if your body gets very relaxed. This leads to mental alertness that puts you in the best position to really see your true essence. Finally, it is important to be upright. When the spine is long and upright, all the muscles of the spine that are meant to relax *can* relax. The nerves coming off the spinal column are free and not crimped in any way. This allows your breathing to be full and relaxed. If you are even slightly bent over or hunched, your belly can't expand, which means the diaphragm – the big sheet of muscle at the bottom of the rib cage – can't fully extend, and the lungs cannot be filled properly. But when your spine is upright, and the belly can expand fully, your breath can be relaxed and easy, unhindered. This by itself has a surprisingly positive effect on the nervous system and on the mind.

It's not hard to get a good posture. When you do, you are well on the way to getting the hang of meditation.

Once you've found a position you want to try from one of these pictures, sit down and make sure your back is upright and truly relaxed. In the pictures the people sitting cross-legged are sitting on at least four inches of support, to help keep their spines upright as well as relaxed. If you try sitting directly on the floor with nothing supporting you, your back muscles will have to work

31

to keep you from rounding your back and to keep you from falling backwards. Over time, your back and body will start to ache. But if you sit on a couple of thick books, a folded pillow or anything you can find, the backbones can stack up correctly, allowing the back muscles to relax.

The spine isn't ramrod straight when it's upright because it's a great piece of engineering with natural curves. This structure, curving slightly in several places – rather than using unnecessary extra muscles and effort – will keep you upright and breathing deeply.

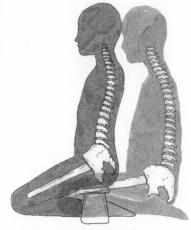

And your spine finds its natural shape when you are sitting high enough, so:

take time to find something, or several things, to sit on so that your bottom is at least four inches off the floor.

People sit on their washing-up bowls, or books softened by folded pillows and blankets. I've sat on a rolled-up pair of jeans, and even stuffed my shoes underneath me at times to add to the height. Of course, if you can lay your hands on a meditation cushion or meditation stool, that's ideal. Or you can make your own: our other free books show you how to make both of these things.

If you are sitting cross-legged or kneeling on the ground, make sure you have a blanket or something similar underneath, including under your feet and ankles, to cushion your joints from the hardness of the floor.

For the Burmese position, bring one foot into the centre, close in towards the body, ankle resting on the floor. Bring the other foot to be just in front of it, with that ankle resting on the floor too.

For the half-lotus, lift one ankle on top of the opposite thigh. Then bring the other foot close in towards the body, ankle resting on the floor.

For the full-lotus, lift one ankle on top of the opposite thigh. Bring the other ankle on top of its opposite thigh too.

For the cross-legged positions, you want your knees to be comfortable. If they don't reach the floor, put something under them, so they can relax. Put just enough support under your knees to rest them, rather than propping them up past their natural stopping point. (Sometimes it's only one knee that doesn't reach the floor which you need to support.) Experiment until you find the right amount of comfort and height. The support needed may change with time and, meanwhile, yoga will help loosen the muscles at the top of your legs, allowing your knees to lower, so you can sit with more comfort.

If you're on a chair or sitting upright with your legs bent off the side of your bed, make sure you sit close to the edge, not leaning back against anything. It can help to have a pillow underneath you, to keep your spine upright.

You have great strength in the back and an ability to support yourself. A quiet, upright pose, with the natural curve of the

Burmese position

Half-lotus position

Full-lotus position

33

spine supporting itself, is a wonderful reflection of who you really are. Your body's uprightness and the natural rhythm of the breath help you to tap into a quiet power, and it is a power which knows that your life is valuable and unique, and that right here is okay. (This might seem miles away from how you feel at the moment. Don't worry. This practice – your practice – is necessary. Just reading about it is like looking at a cup of tea and not tasting it.)

If your chair is low and your knees are higher than your hips, you might become uncomfortable over time, so sit on something like a book or a blanket, so your thighs are level or even sloping slightly downwards towards your knees. If the chair is high, and your toes and heels don't touch the floor, put something under your feet so you feel stable and grounded.

While a meditation stool is ideal for kneeling, you can find lots of things in your cell to help you, like a folded pillow or two, a blanket, and maybe even some clothing which you can slide between your calves, and under your sitting bones (your bottom) until you are high enough to be comfortable. You may then need a little extra padding under the tops of your feet and knees.

The great thing is to experiment with different sitting positions. If you sit for extended periods of time, it's useful to have at least two positions to choose from, for example kneeling and sitting cross-legged. Also, whichever of the Burmese position, half-lotus position or full-lotus position you choose, it's good to alternate the leg and foot that are in front each time you sit, to keep yourself balanced.

Whichever position you are in, make sure the back of your neck is long, like the people in the drawings, with the chin level, not pointing up or down.

Eyes

Keep your eyes open, gazing down past your nose, to a spot on the floor a few feet in front of you. As you begin to tune into your breath, your eyes will probably go out of focus, which is fine. You aren't staring at anything, but instead, your eyes are slightly open and relaxed, blinking naturally from time to time.

Keeping your eyes open is good for a number of reasons. First, you are less likely to become sleepy. Second, with your eyes open, it's far easier to bear in mind that you aren't trying to be somewhere other than right where you are. You aren't trying to create something special inside, or imagine anything. Meditation is about being with what is happening right now, with alertness and stillness, not turning away, or spending time endlessly wishing things to be other than they are.

Perhaps the most important reason is that sometimes sights or sounds around us help us break through our normal way of seeing and understanding, and the smallest thing – a small feather rising and floating out the window, a sweet wrapper crackling on the grass, someone down the hall sneezing – sets off a powerful glimpse into the real truth of our lives as not separate from anything. So when you practise meditation, you are sitting with your eyes resting, cast downwards in front of you, not looking at anything. Meditation is more about responding to an inner attitude of openness, even as you focus on your breathing.

Sometimes in meditation, it's possible to sit for a long time without being aware of seeing or hearing anything. But the world and everything in it is speaking the truth to you, all the time, showing you your deepest self, and sometimes you can really 'get it' in an immediate, unquestionable way. Wanting or anticipating these glimpses, though, only disturbs the mind by setting up discontent with how things are right now. So just keep yourself open to all possibilities with your eyes open, and keep open-minded too!

THE STAIRCASE

What is practising for?
That the innermost nature of everything
may reveal itself to you.

Who shows it to us?
The vegetable,
the staircase,
the window.

Our eyes
do not see it.

But everybody has in them
that which can see IT.

Sylvia Ostertag

Hands

Place your hands like this:

The left hand is on top of the right, and the thumb tips are touching. The hands are resting

in the lap, and the thumbs drawn in towards the belly. Depending on how you are sitting, you may find it useful to have a jumper or small pillow in your lap, to keep your arms from getting tired.

The hands are forming a circle, a symbol pointing towards a truth we can know for ourselves: that we are connected with the entire universe and everything in it. The left side of the body is associated with receptivity and allowing, while the right side is about controlling and ordering. So with this hand position, the quiet side takes precedence over the controlling side, allowing us to simply be with our breath and our lives, just as they are.

It may be that your body won't allow you to kneel or sit upright on the floor or in a chair. A chronic spinal or muscular condition, a temporary bad back, or having to rest while in hospital – these can all mean that you can't sit upright. Don't worry. If you need to lean back or to one side in your wheelchair or a supportive chair, then do that. If the only comfortable position is lying down, lie on your back on your bed or on the floor with a blanket underneath. You may wish to bend the knees and have the soles of your feet flat on the floor or bed, separating the feet enough so the knees rest one against the other. Keeping your eyes open is a must if you lie down, to counter the natural tendency to sleep that comes with this position. Look down the bridge of the nose, rather than straight up at the ceiling.

Remember: Be as comfortable and alert as you can.

What to do with your attention

Your breath is the perfect thing to focus on for meditation. It is as natural as the sky and the breeze. It is neutral, as it doesn't tend to stir up strong emotions. It is quiet, and becomes even quieter as you pay attention to it. It is free. It is inside you. It is connected to your physical body, and the state of your breathing affects your mood and feelings. It will be with you all your life. And breathing is something we share with many other living things. Best of all, you are an expert at it, because you've been doing it since you first drew breath.

When you breathe in, you are taking in the world around you, merging with nitrogen and oxygen and other gases from the air. The oxygen that your cells need to survive can't come from anywhere but outside you. And when you breathe out, you are releasing gases which your body doesn't need, giving a part of yourself back to the world. Breathing quite literally connects inside and outside.

As you meditate, tuning into your breathing, you might discover your curiosity and patience becoming alive. Tuning into your breathing can become such a habit that even when you are not sitting, your attention can rest in the breath, even as you walk along, or eat or talk or listen to other people. And because you are paying attention often with curiosity and patience in seated meditation, these same qualities can come forth naturally in everyday living too, especially when your attention comes back to the breath while doing whatever you are doing.

So there are a few things to sort out before you start. Make your sitting space clear and special. Then look for a good sitting position that suits you. Finally, what do you do with your attention? Start by allowing the body to relax:

1. Take a deep breath in, feeling your belly expand. As you breathe out, let the belly completely relax and let go of as much tension there as you can. Do this three times.

2. Now let your breathing be normal, not artificially deep, and the next time you breathe out, allow all the muscles between your legs to relax, making sure you're not clenching anything.

3. On the out-breath after that, let your thighs relax.

4. Then allow the lower legs to relax on your out-breath. Then the feet. Use each out-breath to help yourself let go

of holding tension in the body. You may start to feel how the breath and mind can work together to help the body.

5. Think about your shoulders and arms and let them relax too, using the breath.

6. Let your forehead and face be easy and soft.

7. Relax the throat and slightly, very slightly, drop the chin.

8. Finally, be aware of your physical presence, of your body just sitting. Feel yourself in touch with the chair, or cushion or whatever you're sitting on. Feel where your feet are in contact with the floor. Notice the weight of your arms hanging from your shoulders, and notice your hands in your lap, with the thumb tips touching. Enjoy the length in the back of your neck and be aware of your uprightness, and each of its natural curves. Then, for half a minute or so, sit and breathe with an overall sense of simply sitting here.

Now begin to tune into your breath, breathing in and out naturally through your nose. If it's blocked for some reason, then of course breathe through your mouth. The air is cleaned of germs, warmed, and slightly moistened if you breathe through your nose, so it's in the best possible condition to be used by your body when it reaches your lungs.

Counting the in-breaths and out-breaths

Breathe normally and as naturally as you can, and then begin counting the breath. On the in-breath, say silently in your mind, '1'. On the out-breath, say silently '2'. On the next in-breath, '3'. On the following out-breath, '4'. Keep going like this, up to 10. When you get to 10, start again at 1. If you lose your way, it doesn't matter a single bit. Just start again at 1.

COUNTING JUST THE OUT-BREATHS

Another way, which takes more concentration, is to count only the out-breaths. When you breathe in, feel the breath coming into

39

the body, and when you breathe out, say '1' to yourself silently. Breathe in in total silence, just aware of the breath and body, and as you breathe out say '2' in your mind. Keep going up to 10, and start again at 1.

Being the breath

Still more challenging is simply being aware of the breath, letting yourself be the breath. With this way, there is no counting. There is just allowing the breath to happen, and feeling the body naturally expand as the breath comes in, and feeling it relax as the breath goes out.

When you breathe in, air passes over the upper lip and over the rims of the nostrils. Can you feel that passage of air there? It moves through the throat, and the chest expands, and the belly too as the in-breath happens. Can you feel the breath in the throat, and feel the belly and chest expanding?

As you breathe out, the belly relaxes, and the chest too. The air moves out of the throat, out of the nostrils and across the upper lip. It's possible to be aware of the breath in all of these areas, in such a way that there isn't a big sense of you watching the breath, or even of it happening to you. Instead, it's just: breathing going on and attention resting in that breathing.

If your attention on the breath absorbs you and focusing in the whole body breathing seems too busy, then just focus on the rim of the nostrils, or the upper lip just under the nose, where you can feel air passing in and out. This will sharpen your concentration further.

Whether counting the breath or being the breath, be aware of the space that happens at the end of your out-breath, before you start to breathe in again. Nothing is happening here, in this space. Allow this gap to be. Don't rush through it, and don't hang on to it. Just include it in your awareness of the whole breath. Be with the stillness here in this space. You'll notice there's a similar space at the end of the in-breath, before you start breathing out. While it may not seem quite as restful and empty-feeling, you can also notice that space. Whether you are counting the breath, or simply being with the breath, appreciate these spaces, and let the next part of the breath begin in its own time, naturally. With attention very finely attuned to the whole of the breath, can breathing just happen, without very much 'me' in it? In the end you stop noting the spaces and simply become absorbed in your natural breathing.

When to do it and for how long

The first thing after waking in the morning is a good time to sit in meditation. The mind hasn't become very active or involved with the day yet. Not having eaten breakfast, your body's energy isn't tied up with digestion. (Yes, digestion takes energy. It's an extreme example, but consider how sleepy you are after a heavy meal.) And your surroundings will be quieter, the earlier you get up. Many people in prison say they meditate before the rest of the prison wakes up. Some who share a cell even rise and prepare themselves silently, without disturbing their sleeping cellmate.

Sometime before going to bed for the night is another good time. If you aren't too tired, you might choose to do it immediately before sleeping. Meditating at this time definitely helps you sleep more soundly; sleeping is a problem for a lot of people, whether they're in prison or not. Also, this time of day can bring with it a reassuring sense that there's nothing else that needs to be done. (By the way, not watching TV in the hour or so before you turn in for the night will improve your sleep. So will going to sleep at roughly the same time each night.)

But your circumstances may be different. Maybe you find your cellmate very noisy or difficult, and think it may be impossible to meditate when they are there, but there are times during the day when they are out, and you can choose those times. In time too, you may realise that if you become comfortable doing it when they're around, they get used to it too, especially if you can find a way to do it while sitting on your bed, completely in your own space. Occasionally, people have found that their cellmate becomes interested too and they start to sit together.

41

'I have persuaded my pad mate (no new age follower of yoga, I assure you) to give it a whirl and we have had about half a dozen sessions doing the relaxation and meditation. On a couple of occasions he has even instigated them himself! Because we are both British and of a certain age it can be a little awkward, but once we get over our straight-laced disposition, we both get value from it. He, like me, can talk for England, and therefore 40 minutes in silence and meditation from both of us is quite an achievement. And very beneficial.'

Calum, HMP Risley

So how long should you sit for? Start with an amount of time that does not overwhelm you. (I wouldn't recommend starting on your own with a whole weekend!) You could try just five minutes three times a day if you like. This is only a little bit longer than an advert break on the telly, which most people manage to sit through, no problem.

Image by Darren

If you have an alarm on your clock or watch, you can set it for the amount of time you've chosen, and then forget completely about time and focus on the breathing. It's harder without an alarm, as you may continuously want to check the time. But there are other ways. For example, if you want to sit for 25 minutes, and your neighbour's telly *always* blasts out the *Coronation Street* theme tune at 7.30, then start at 7.05, with the music marking the end of your sit.

The benefits of meditation don't always come quickly. Like any new skill, it takes time and patience to develop. So try meditating for five minutes, three times a day. Do this for four or five days, and then perhaps go up to ten minutes on one of those sits, and sticking with five on the other two. After four or five more days, maybe you want to increase the two five-minute periods to ten minutes, so you're meditating three times a day, for ten minutes each time.

Because all of us are different, with different daily schedules and different levels of motivation and interest, you will have to experiment for yourself on the amount of time. But have some faith in the early days, knowing that you will start to feel a difference before too long. Just so you know, when you sit for 20 minutes minimum there's a chemical change in the body as stress levels drop along with the pulse rate, while the waves of the brain also become less agitated and more peaceful.

While there are some general principles, there is no right and wrong when it comes to when you should meditate, or how long you should do it for each time. You must figure out for yourself what works for you at this point in your life. From time to time, as your circumstances change, you might make some changes. Add on ten minutes, or do it later in the morning, or do one longer period instead of two shorter ones.

'I took up…meditation again about three weeks ago and have found it is a great way to de-stress… I feel better now that I'm practising again. Though I was quite meditative in my walking and conscious of others and my environment,

> I feel the actual sitting meditation needs to be done. It's been enjoyable but also helped me through some difficult memories. I remember that meditation is not about feeling happy all the time. It is about living in the moment.'
>
> *Baz, Rowanbank Clinic*

After a few days, weeks or months of meditating regularly, you may find it's become a habit, a normal part of what you do each day. Still, there may be times when you think, 'I've got better things to do.' That programme on the telly about penguins or the compelling serial you are watching. Or you want to write home. This happens to us all. It takes a little bit of talking yourself around to actually stop what you're doing, and go to your cushion or chair and to sit. Once you're there, it's no problem, and you can sit for the whole time you've given yourself. New habits are not always easy, but not impossible either.

Excuses for not sitting may sound something like this: I'm too tired, it's too late in the evening. I need to phone or write to my wife. (Actually you are in a far better mood and better company if your meditation practice is regular: the quality of being with other people gets so much better.) I feel upset, or sick, or out of sorts, so I'm not going to be able to focus anyway. I'd be better off sleeping. What's the point in sitting still doing nothing? My time would be better spent organising this or that aspect of my life.

Your excuses will be unique to you, but perhaps you can see a common theme: we don't see the value in meditating, and other things seem more important. Obviously, if a friend is in deep distress and needs to talk, you want to give them some attention. If you've got a test or a meeting coming up and you need to prepare for it, that's important (though having made some time to meditate earlier in the day will help you to stay focussed *in* the meeting *and* to be fully present for your friend).

It's funny, but really, finding the time and space to meditate is easy. It's something that you simply learn to value. At times when you feel resistance to it, you have to trust that it's worth doing.

That's when it takes some self-discipline. It's completely normal to experience these periods.

Remembering Etty Hillesum's words may be useful when you don't feel like sitting. Etty was a Jew living in Nazi-occupied Holland, where many in her community were slowly disappearing each day to the concentration camps to be gassed. These are the worst conditions any of us can imagine, not least because Etty herself knew that her own time was limited. Yet she found a deep sense of meaning and beauty in life by learning to go inside herself and finding silence there. In *An Interrupted Life*, she wrote 'Ultimately, we have just one moral duty: to reclaim large areas of peace in ourselves, more and more peace, and to reflect it towards others. And the more peace there is in us, the more peace there will also be in our troubled world.' So you can remind yourself sometimes, 'Even though I don't feel like sitting today, perhaps it is one way that I can create more peace in this world.'

Sitting for longer periods

Being still and focusing on the breath in meditation for 25 minutes or longer brings some great benefits. It is often only after 25 minutes that the mind seems to really slow down, and it's possible to sense the stillness and power which comes from sustained concentration. Also, this length of time gives you a chance to learn how to deal with all the distractions that come up. They do come up. That's part of the 'practice' part of meditation practice. It's only by giving yourself enough time with the distractions that this learning happens. There's no short cut through them or way to get around them. It's only by being with them over longer periods of time that your own experience shows you that their power can lessen and your focus and attention can become stronger.

If at some point you choose to meditate for an hour at a time, or longer, it's useful to break up the sitting with walking meditation. It's usual in some meditation traditions to sit for 25 minutes, then walk for five minutes then sit again for 25, and so on. The walking keeps the body from becoming stiff, but equally important, it is a chance to continue meditating while you walk

45

without breaking your concentration. While you will be aware of the floor touching your feet, and the movement of your body, you can keep your attention grounded in your in-breath and out-breath, eyes cast down, returning the attention to your breath counting or being with the breath when attention wanders, just as you do when you are sitting. After five minutes, you can sit again.

The speed you walk for meditation should be slower than normal walking speed, but not super-slow. It's more like the pace of strolling with a friend, engaged in deep conversation, only you are engaged with the breath. Not walking to get anywhere. Just be with each step and each breath, and let everything else go.

If you are doing this in your cell, you simply walk slowly back and forth, aware of each step and aware of turning around before walking again. Your meditation is continuing seamlessly from sitting. If by some chance you are doing this outside, you might be able to walk in a large circle, so that you don't have to turn around.

As you walk, you can clasp your hands lightly behind your back, arms hanging down. Especially if you are out in the open with other people who aren't meditating, this position is good: it looks more normal, so it shouldn't attract attention. If you are alone, or with a group that is meditating together, you can hold your hands in front of you, with the fingers of the right hand wrapped around the right thumb, so it makes a tight fist, and the left hand covering the right. The hands are held next to the body, at the lower end of the breastbone. This position really helps you gather and focus your energy.

CHAPTER 3

The Right Approach

The previous chapter was all about what to do when you meditate. This one is about principles that may help keep you on track. But really, there's only one thing you need to keep in mind as you approach sitting:

just sit.

Often, people who are starting out can do this easily. They have the joy of a 'beginner's mind', one that's free of ideas, and so they slip easily into the simplicity of meditation. Being a beginner like this is a very fortunate place to be. Try to keep it simple.

The benefits of regularly immersing yourself in meditation include freedom, acceptance and responsibility. Freedom here means greater ease with life, getting along more harmoniously with yourself and your circumstances. Acceptance means not resisting what is, which leads back to a kind of freedom too: freedom from the need or compulsion to make things different, or feel upset that they're the way they are. And responsibility is the capacity to find just the right response to what might be going on without even trying, and your ability to respond appropriately is a wonderful offshoot of meditation.

You probably know the phrase, 'Start as you mean to go on', which means when you begin something new, adopt the principles that you really believe are effective. Do this with meditation, and you can't go wrong. Each time you sit down, you can bring acceptance of what is, a sense of freedom, and responsibility to your whole being.

Acceptance

Acceptance is perhaps the easiest to understand. Say your attention is all over the place as you are meditating, and just won't stay still. As you try to count your breath, you can't move beyond, '1...2...3... I'm so tired... Oh, I've wandered off: 1...2... Wonder what's for tea... Oh! Back to my breath: 1...2...3...4...5... I think I'm getting the hang of this meditation. Maybe I'll go into some advanced state soon. Oh, wandering again: 1...2...' That's how it is at the moment. Accept that your mind is like that and stick with it, gently returning your attention to your breath and to counting each time you realise it's wandered off.

Acceptance is about not trying to change anything or make yourself or anything else better. It's about allowing it all to happen. There is just this fact of what is going on, and acceptance means that it's all okay. In the book *Zen Mind, Beginner's Mind*,[1] the author likens this to giving a cow or sheep a huge field, rather than trying to control it. This is the best kind of control. It sounds easy, just to let your thoughts come and go, like a cow in a vast, fenceless field, without being bothered by what it does. But it's not easy, and it takes a special kind of effort, which each person has to develop for themselves.

Freedom

Freedom is related to acceptance, because you are letting aspects of the mind just be free. You're not trying to change them. Yes, you

---

1   Shunryu Suzuki. *Zen Mind, Beginner's Mind*. New York: Weatherhill, 1970.

have chosen to make time in your day to sit down and meditate. Yes, you are sitting still, with real determination and focus. And yes, you are choosing to keep up the practice of returning your attention again and again and again to the breath, which takes effort. But you are free in that you aren't caught up in getting it right or not getting it right; in having a quiet mind or not having a quiet mind. Really, none of that matters, as you just keep kindly and gently returning to your breath. So you can start with freedom from the need to get anywhere or do anything or change anything about yourself.

The other aspect of freedom when it comes to sitting, is the benefit of coming to sit with a body and a nervous system that is more relaxed, calm and alert, through having practised yoga or some other form of movement and awareness. Yoga can lend stability to your heart and mind so that when distractions arise, you can return attention to the breath with only the tiniest effort. You may even find yourself twitching less. Occasionally, you might feel so relaxed in your body and mind that you feel like you could sit forever. Don't overlook this fact that yoga postures and movements help you to sit in meditation with great stillness and focus.

Responsibility

Choosing to focus on the breath instead of what is distracting is not denying or repressing anything. It's taking responsibility for how the mind behaves, and what you choose to focus on. It strengthens the mind's ability to stay steady and accepting. With determination and acceptance of exactly what's going on, it's possible to be with almost everything that arises in meditation, to take responsibility for how the mind is. This doesn't mean giving yourself a hard time. It means simply being with it. You may have to repeatedly, for the whole period that you are sitting, bring your attention away from what is distracting you, again and again. Still other times, you may become quiet and focused to the point where distractions barely register before dying away.

49

If you are someone who experiences flashbacks or other symptoms from post-traumatic stress disorder, should you try to meditate when you are having a flashback? No. But you'll probably find that having a meditation practice (and doing it in 'normal' times) helps decrease the intensity and frequency of your PTSD symptoms.

But if after a long period of trying to stay focused on your breathing, your thoughts or feelings become so powerful that they seem to be completely dominating you – really strong sadness or self-doubt for example – stay right there. Ask yourself: 'How does this sadness make my breathing? How is the breath? How do my joints feel? How is my belly? How is my posture when I'm like this? And what does it do to the tone of my mind?' Stick with the feeling and see how it affects your breath, your body and your mental tone. To fully experience what it is to be sad, right now, without judgement or wishing it away. This is not denying sadness: it is experiencing it fully. If you stay with it long enough, you can see through it. You can do this with sadness, doubt, anger or any feeling that's dominating you. That is a wonderful way to respond, to take responsibility.

But just a reminder of the most important principle:

*the fewer ideas that you have when you actually
sit down to meditate, the better.*

No need for change

Almost everyone gets interested in meditation because they want to change. Most of us feel dissatisfied with some part of ourselves. We're looking for some way of making things different, making ourselves better, changing our lives, changing the way we feel. This might be your motivation for sitting. It is a completely normal and natural reason to start meditating.

There's something that's back to front here. On the one hand I'm suggesting there's no need to change, but on the other hand, just doing meditation is an attempt to change your life. This puzzle is one that you may find yourself working with for a long time: meaningful change only happens when you fully accept how you are right now, and are fully *in your life just as it is*, rather than hanging on to some idea of how you think you should be! A man named Arnold Beisser, a Gestalt therapist,[2] spelled this out in his paradoxical theory of change. It goes like this:

> Change occurs when one becomes what he is, not when he tries to become what he is not. Change does not take place through a coercive attempt by the individual or by another person to change him, but it does take place if one takes the time and effort to be what he is – to be fully invested in his current positions. By rejecting the role of change agent, we make meaningful and orderly change possible.

Meditation is brilliant at working with this truth. In order for the heart and mind to become still and focused, you really do have to give up all attempts at changing anything, and simply accept things as they are as you sit. This goes for everything, from an irritating piece of music that you can't get out of your head, to some deeply held belief about yourself, to the fact that your mind is racing around, full of thoughts and ideas. The more you fight and resist how things are at this moment as you sit, the less you are able to focus.

But with patience and time, you develop the capacity to be with what you don't like, and what you wish you could change, whether that's a noisy mind or environment or an aspect of yourself or your behaviour. Somehow, focusing on the breath with wordless attention over a period of time gives you the capacity to let these things simply be, without needing to claim them as yours, nor make them go away. Instead, if they are simply allowed to be there, without reacting to them one way or another, they

---

2   Gestalt is an experiential form of psychotherapy with a strong focus upon the individual's experience in the present moment.

begin to lose their power. Depending on what you are struggling to accept, it may eventually lose its power, sometimes over a matter of minutes, or weeks – or it may take years of practice.

The more that you can accept and be with yourself fully – just as you are – the more that 'meaningful and orderly change' begins to happen. This change is not something that you can predict, and it can come spontaneously, without any planning. The letters in the second part of this book are full of examples of this kind of change.

I hope you get some moments of this not-trying-to-change-anything as you meditate. Perhaps after striving and struggling for a while, you'll find things becoming quiet and you notice the breath is quiet too and is simply happening on its own. Everything is unfolding just as it should and you are in touch with something still and silent and all-embracing that allows everything to be exactly as it is. At those times, just continue to let go as much as you can into the wordless silence as you fully inhabit the breath.

'Recently I actually let go while meditating... What an experience. Totally liberating and freeing. The same night and next day I was so full of love, it felt like every drop of love in the universe was coursing through every single molecule of my body. It did not stay with me for long, but... I'm okay with that. I just enjoyed it while it lasted.'

John, HMP Wayland

Soft and alert

It's worth remembering that this practice is not easy, although it can be quite simple. Our minds are used to wandering as they wish. Restlessness and continual movement are habitual for us. So we need to bring tremendous alertness and develop sharp attention on the breath, if we aren't to get side-tracked by thoughts. Think of the alertness and concentration of a tiger, watching intensely

as it stalks, before springing into action. While you may make meditation part of your daily routine, the practice itself shouldn't become routine. Your alertness needs to be strong and fresh, like the tiger's, even if you've sat for tens of thousands of hours. Each moment is totally new. Your upright sitting position will let you welcome it, just as it is.

At the same time, you need to bring tremendous softness. There's no need to change anything about yourself, no need to resist or respond to the distractions inside or outside, no need to hold any tightness in the body. Meditation is not about forcing something to happen that you want to happen. All we seek and desire in our deepest heart is already here. Bringing tremendous softness to each breath allows us to see that.

Alertness and softness may seem like contradictory qualities, but you will see for yourself that they aren't. You can consciously bring them both to each breath. Can you see how they are right

53

here with this out-breath, the space afterwards, this in-breath, this pause? And they will develop and deepen with time, becoming stronger mental habits the more you use them.

When your alertness is strong, and when you bring great softness too, gradually – or perhaps suddenly – what you think you know about yourself and the world starts to fade. Ideas and notions about all kinds of things loosen their hold, and rather than *thinking* about your experience, you are simply...experiencing. Somehow, everything you know is forgotten, or put aside. As with softness and alertness, you can start as you mean to go on: try not to bring any preconceived ideas with you – about anything – as you sit.

'I don't meditate to be free of anything. In my earlier years, maybe. But in that state of oneness (I don't even like the term oneness – it implies a twoness) there is no concept of anything... I don't sit down for meditation and decide, "Right. Today I'm going to have a real deep, long session." If I tried that, the effort would become a hindrance. I just sit.'

Darren, HMP Wakefield

What is it like not to know anything as you pay attention to each breath? To be without a past, to have no framework to explain things? Not to rely on any of the knowledge you've accumulated in your lifetime? This might sound far out, impossible, or scary. But in fact we all have brief moments in ordinary life when the mind is set free from everything that it knows, and those moments can actually bring an intense peace and satisfaction. With meditation, we are merely cultivating that natural capacity of our minds and hearts and bringing it more into our everyday life.

It's not all about 'me'

The last principle to mention is that meditation practice is not just about 'me' and what 'I' can get out of it. You are connected to every single other thing in the universe. It's easy to see that we human beings are influenced by the things we read, the people who were around when we were growing up and the kind of food we eat, to name just a few factors. We are completely dependent on the sun, which keeps our planet warm and makes possible the growth of plants, which ultimately keep us alive. We are sustained and affected in a deep and profound way by a countless number of other things and processes.

But the influence isn't one-way. We too have a profound effect on the world around us, and on other people. Most of the time, you may not stop to think about this influence, or appreciate how deep it is. And it isn't merely *what* you do – like helping someone learn to read and write, or making a cup of tea for a new arrival, or serving as a Listener. It's *how* you do it. It's the fundamental stance you take towards your experience, towards yourself and other people which has such an impact. Meditation has a profound effect on this stance. So as you approach each breath, know that it is not just this body and mind of yours that is benefiting. It is in fact everyone and everything that you come into contact with.

There are people who choose to live alone in caves or huts or cells for long periods of their lives, devoted only to meditation and to deepening their experience of life in each moment, or for some people, touching the sacred. It might sound crazy, but these people too are benefiting the whole of the universe, despite having little or no contact with other humans.

You are part of a vast and unified field that contains everything. As you sit with this in-breath and this out-breath, know that it is for the benefit of the whole of creation that you bring yourself back when attention wanders, and when you cultivate alertness and softness with the breath. Everything in the universe is being helped as you let go of your ideas about yourself.

The ironic thing is this: the less your practice is about you and what you can get from it, the richer and fuller life becomes. But even to practise for a fuller and richer life is not exactly right. Just sit: not for you, not for the universe.

CHAPTER 4

Distractions in Meditation

'Make me one with everything, please.'

All this talk about unity and being one with the universe is great. But the fact is, after you have been sitting for some time, distractions will arise, and you will probably feel *anything but* peaceful and focused. This is completely normal, so please don't feel you're getting it wrong. In fact, distractions and learning how to be with them is a really vital part of meditation.

Buddhists have a useful way of explaining distractions in meditation. (You don't have to be a Buddhist to make use of this understanding, any more than you have to be Italian to enjoy pizza.) There are five kinds of distractions and they happen to everyone at some time or another:

1. *Sleepiness* – when you are either on the edge of sleep, or you are actually asleep – maybe even dreaming – or the mind is just sluggish and heavy. In any case, your breathing is completely forgotten because of the drowsiness.

2. *Desire* – when the mind is fixed on an object or outcome that it wants. There is some activity in the mind to pull what it craves closer, or move towards it, or considering this thing or outcome while wanting it. It is common for the mind to become calmer or to slow down, and this calmer state can itself become something you start to crave. Or it may be a desire for time to pass, or the desire to change yourself, or have someone in your life behave differently towards you.

3. *Aversion* – the opposite of desire, as the mind attempts to push away or get rid of something. This can range from mild irritation, to anger, to a burning, all-consuming hatred.

4. *Restlessness* – when the mind is whirring and churning about something, maybe planning some future event, or replaying a past event. It could be developing some system of thought or logic to explain something about yourself, or the universe, or a traffic flow system or a better designed yoga mat. It can also include worry, or being thrown off focus by an external noise. The point is, the mind is fluttering about, or flapping quite hard, and the mind is drawn away from merely paying attention to the breath to a line of thought that is characterised by worry or restlessness.

5. *Doubt* – a feeling of doubt about yourself, about what you are doing as you meditate, or the validity of meditation itself. It's good to have a healthy scepticism towards any practice, but once you've examined and considered something before trying it and decided it's worth a go, doubt can move from being a useful tool to an obstacle.

THE GUEST HOUSE

This being human is a guest house.
Every morning a new arrival.

A joy, a depression, a meanness,
some momentary awareness comes
As an unexpected visitor.

Welcome and entertain them all!
Even if they're a crowd of sorrows,
who violently sweep your house
empty of its furniture,
still treat each guest honorably.
He may be clearing you out
for some new delight.

The dark thought, the shame, the malice,
meet them at the door laughing,
and invite them in.

Be grateful for whoever comes,
because each has been sent
as a guide from beyond.

Mewlana Jalaluddin Rumi,
13th-century Sufi mystic

The reason for pointing out these obstacles to the mind becoming focused is to reassure you. If you know they are a common feature for *everyone* who meditates, they may lose some of their sting or power. You may find that naming each distraction as it appears helps you return your focus to the breathing. But be careful not to turn 'naming' into an exercise. Remember, you are simply trying to allow things to be, without controlling or analysing or doing anything with them, developing concentration on the breath.

These five categories are general descriptions of complex mental activities, which are sometimes not so easy to pin down. It may be that there is more than one of these activities going on. Desire may be mixed in with restlessness, for example.

As far as possible, do not treat anything as annoyances or something you are doing wrong. Getting cross or thinking you're doing it wrong muddies the waters even more. As much as possible, let thoughts or feelings be, without giving them any energy. Let all your attention go to the breathing in and the breathing out. Let thoughts just come and let them go. This approach sounds easy, but it requires special effort. Distractions force you to discover for yourself how to make this special effort, so ultimately they can be empowering, annoying as they may seem!

A note on noise

Prisons are noisy, and noise may bring up so much aversion in you when trying to meditate that it makes you give up in a huff. Understandable! A telly, someone else's music, shouting, loud banter, doors slamming, keys jangling – all this can really grate. The human voice seems especially distracting while you're trying to sit.

The good news is that if you can hang in there with it just as it is, your concentration and absorption will improve and something just might shift.

The other day when I was meditating there was a radio on next door, a talking programme blaring out loud and clear. I stayed still, trying to tune into my breath, but kept following the voices and the ideas on the radio. Then I thought about the colossal noise challenge in prisons. That helped me get some perspective on my situation, and gave me a little distance from the frustration. In the past I've used meditation when in intense pain so I decided to apply the same principles: stick right here and breathe into what is hard and unpleasant (it's not going to kill you). Be curious about it.

Gradually I started to notice my reactions. I noticed what kind of expectations I had about how my mind *should* be feeling. Noticing these things, I could let them go, a little bit at a time. After about 20 minutes, I stopped being so reactive to the words of the human voices and could keep fairly continually focused on the breathing. Getting up after another ten minutes and starting to talk to people and continuing my day, I felt clearer and more open and ready for whatever might happen next, which is how I often feel after meditating in a quiet place.

You'll hear time and time again in the letters in the second part that it is only by being with what is hard, rather than running away or trying to eliminate it, that people manage to find any satisfaction. This gives them new respect for themselves and what they are capable of. By learning to be with the inevitable obstacles in meditation, you strengthen your capacity to be with even bigger challenges.

CHAPTER 5

Meditation in Day-to-Day Life

Sitting still, counting or being with your breath, or doing walking meditation may be hard, but at least the instructions are clear: notice when your attention has drifted and then return to your breath.

Living the rest of your day in a way that develops and nurtures your heart and mind can be more of a challenge. When you get up from sitting and the cell door opens, there are far more choices about what to do with your time and attention. So how can you keep a meditative approach to the whole of your day, the whole of your life?

Waking up to life: coming off autopilot

In the early days of aeroplanes, the pilot had control over every single movement the plane made. On today's passenger jets, there is very little that the pilots have to do for much of the flight: they can put the plane on automatic pilot, leaving it up to computer systems without even having to be aware of what is happening.

One way to think about how to live your life moment to moment is to ask yourself: right now, am I living this moment on autopilot, or am I moving and thinking with awareness? Maybe you have a cup of tea with you as you are reading this. The next time you take a sip, notice that it's possible to feel the impulse to take a sip, to take a decision to actually have a drink, to be aware of your hand moving towards the mug or cup, to feel the warmth and weight and texture of it as you take hold of it, to know that you are moving it towards your mouth, to notice the taste of the tea as you sip it, and to be aware of replacing the cup back where it was resting. Feel the warmth of the tea in your throat as you swallow.

It's also possible to drink your tea on autopilot, without being very aware of what's happening, to speed through it, with the idea in the back of your mind that there's somewhere else you need to be, or some point in the future that's better, or holds more promise. Being on autopilot means that you miss out on what's happening, like walking hurriedly down the road without noticing the warmth of the sun on your skin, or the movement of the breeze. In prison there may appear to be far more negative than positive things, which makes it more important to remember to bring your full attention to the pleasant occurrences like enjoying a glass of water, sharing a laugh with someone, the taste of tea, the pleasure of having a shower or brushing your teeth. This helps you feel more connection to what's around you, and consequently, a connection to your own life.

Sometimes life feels absolutely hell and you don't want to be with what's happening, or with your own memories. Our bodies and minds have developed coping mechanisms to shield us from overwhelming experiences and memories where we do, in effect, take ourselves out of our own lives and go on autopilot. At times, we can find ourselves reacting irrationally, often violently, to something that reminds us of a past event. These are completely understandable reactions. Or you may have times when you literally feel you're living in the past.

If you are continually reliving unpleasant memories, and flipping out at minor events, or living on autopilot to try to avoid what is unpleasant, look back at the breathing exercises in Chapter 2. The movements and postures of yoga can also help restore a sense of safety, calm, and trust in life and in your own body, so that you can start to inhabit the present moment, memories and all. If you are lucky enough to be able to do this in a group setting like a prison yoga or meditation class, where a sense of trust in other people is restored too, so much the better.

Much of the time, many people live on autopilot out of habit. Regular sitting meditation gently helps you to understand attention and how it can be cultivated, and it teaches you how the mind tends to wander. It teaches the difference between living life awake versus asleep. And it helps bring attention to the rest of your day.

In the same way that you bring attention back to the breath in seated meditation when you notice the mind has wandered, it's possible to come off autopilot in the rest of your day whenever you remember to. That might be when you are drinking tea, or it might be when you are getting dressed, or walking through your cell door onto the wing. Any time you're in action is an opportunity to bring attention to what you are doing, to be awake to your life. You can even sit on the toilet with awareness.

If you buy the idea that it might be worthwhile to try to pay attention to your life in each moment, whenever you remember to, there's another idea to consider that goes along with the first one: right here, right now, is the most important moment in your life. And allowing yourself to be fully with everything that is happening in this moment is the ultimate way of paying respect to yourself, to the universe, to your higher power if you have one. It's a perfect form of worship. What would that be like if it were true? What's it like to try living right here, right now for even ten minutes, or half a day?

You know from your own experience that it's possible to be aware of your body, breath, surroundings, feelings and thoughts as you move. You can also do this throughout the day when you have periods of stillness. So, for example, you can look up from the page now

—————— ❧ ——————

EVERYDAY LIFE

*To practise
in everyday life
in accordance with
an inner way
nothing is needed
other than quiet attention
directed at
what is going on
just now.*

*Walking.
Shaking hands.
Drinking water.*

Sylvia Østertag

—————— ❧ ——————

and notice the detail of the wall nearest you. Like in meditation, can you bring attention, curiosity, and your full presence to just being here? You are just seeing what you are seeing, hearing what you are hearing, feeling your body in contact with the bed or chair or floor or wall, and feeling the breath moving in the body.

There are lots of times throughout the day when nothing is happening, when you're waiting for something to happen. Maybe you're waiting in the dinner queue, or for someone to show up for an appointment. Rather than these being annoying delays, can they be opportunities to pay attention? To ground yourself, noticing impatience and paying full attention to the breath as you notice colours, sights, sounds, smells? As you continue to stay grounded in the breathing, to see how you feel, to notice the tone in your heart and mind? And just as in seated meditation, to allow, not force anything to change, but simply be with it all?

Who am I when not thinking about me?

As you pause at these times when nothing is happening, and take the chance to be here fully in your life, can you let go of ideas of an 'I' who is doing this, or a 'me' who this is happening to? Can you simply let experience happen? Are there times throughout the day when the ordinary human habit of thinking about yourself is very quiet, or perhaps stopped altogether, because you have taken attention into the breath and to what is happening in and around you, and there is a simpler kind of experiencing?

The day is absolutely overflowing with opportunities to pay attention, to be fully alive to life – the life that is you, and the life that is around you – and the interactions between it all. Paying attention to the breath brings forward a certain inner stillness and silence, and the more you become familiar with this silence, rather than operating on autopilot, the richer life seems.

The world around is speaking, wordlessly, all the time, revealing something beyond our small mind. Dropping everything and simply being with what is in front of us can shift us out of a narrow, constricted feeling we have about life. Do you really see the empty bench with sun and shadow on it and what it has to show? What's it like to just be the leaves moving in the breeze? To let the crow's 'Kaw! Kaw!' ring unfiltered in our bones? To drop away at the sound of someone hanging up the phone receiver outside your cell?

This is by no means to say that you should give up your interests, abandon talking, and try to stop your imagination. Most definitely not. It is not a choice between paying attention and cultivating silence on the one hand and pursuing your interests and getting involved in activities on the other hand. Writing, drawing, talking with others, doing courses you are interested in (and doing courses you *have* to do) – these can all be nourishing.

What matters though is that whether your day is busy with lots of time out of your cell, or whether you are banged up for 23 hours, there is no moment when you can't pay attention.

Linking yoga and meditation

Some people enjoy using their bodies as a way of developing more awareness and focus. Certain activities such as yoga, while not the same as formal, seated meditation, are nonetheless *meditative*: a chance to focus and to cultivate inner silence. If you are drawn to yoga, it's worth looking at the role of attention and the breath in yoga practice.

When you are in a yoga posture, it is completely possible to keep your attention on your breathing, even as you are aware of muscles working, of body parts moving, and of physical sensations, pleasant and unpleasant. In fact, keeping your attention on your breathing as you hold postures or move in a sequence helps increase awareness of your body, and of your thoughts and feelings. Sometimes people will say, 'I'm no good at yoga. I can't touch my toes.' But in fact, being good at yoga is knowing what you are doing

67

as you do it, no matter how simple or complex the movement or posture. Could it be that brushing your teeth is yoga, if done with full awareness as you breathe in and breathe out? Could it be that standing on your head for ten minutes is not yoga, if it's done for showing off or to build up your image of how great you are, with little attention paid to the breath, the mind or physical sensations?

The best and most helpful yoga classes I've been to are the ones where the teachers are comfortable with the students simply returning to their breath as they work, where they offer plenty of reminders to do that, and where they don't over-emphasise achieving a particular shape. Instead they help the students use the breath to deepen awareness of the body, the mind, and the silence and stillness to be found within movement, or as we hold a posture for a long time.

This point is really vital: that befriending the breath throughout the day in whatever we are doing, becoming intimate with it so that it is with us more and more of the time, helps us to trust ourselves and to live more and more from that place of inner silence that the breath helps reveal.

Also, no matter how little free time it seems you have, make time each day for seated meditation. Sitting still committed to your breath, with nothing else to do, is an opportunity to sharpen the mind's attention in a way that is unmatched when you are up and moving around.

Whether you're just starting with meditation, or have been doing it for many years, have faith in your determination and courage. Also, make use of any support you can find in prison to share and talk about what's going on in your practice – a friend or like-minded prisoner, someone in the chaplaincy, or even writing to us at the Prison Phoenix Trust. You may be surprised how much people learn from you, and how your experience can help others.

If you're interested in what meditation can offer, reading about how to do it and about other people's experiences can take you only so far. If you don't sit down and do it yourself, it's like reading the menu in a restaurant but not eating anything. Be sure to taste for yourself!

PART II

Letters

At the Prison Phoenix Trust, we learn all the time from friends inside. You could say that you teach us everything we need to know. That knowledge is worth sharing. So in this section, you'll meet people like yourself. With their freedom taken away and facing *all kinds* of struggles – with prison bureaucracy, with their past, with their families on the outside, and with themselves – they were drawn to meditation. Some started out of curiosity; others because they were bored or desperate. Still others started with a sense of finally 'coming home'. Their stories are all taken from letters written to the Prison Phoenix Trust over the years. Most are written from prison or secure hospitals, but some are from people who have served their time and are now living on the outside once again.

The letters naturally fall into groups like Love, Hope and Gratitude, but you'll see that these themes run through many of the letters. While every person who writes to us gets a reply, we haven't always included replies here. Some replies are very brief, because we've only chosen those parts that support the purpose of this book: the original letters are often much longer. Readers who have had little contact with prisons may come across unfamiliar words or phrases, so we've included 'Some Prison Terms Explained' towards the back.

You may wish to read only a few letters at a time, so you can properly absorb whatever message is coming across to you. As you reflect on each person's experience, you can check and see if there's anything that you can apply in your own life and your own meditation practice. Often people start writing down their own thoughts and experiences after reading personal accounts like these, and you may find that's useful for you to do.

But the letters may absorb you in a more general way as you step into the lives of the writers, and you find your natural empathy rising. Or you might simply find yourself amazed or stunned by what people are going through.

Whatever happens, I hope you find these letters inspiring.

Anger

Anger can absolutely overwhelm you at times, hijacking your life. Even when you have some awareness of your own anger and the problems it causes, it may still have an irresistible pull. Many people, like Darren who writes later in this section, have written about the corrosive effects of anger on their bodies, and their lives.

If we know that it's so damaging, why do we continue to 'do anger'? One friend in prison wrote that he used anger to protect himself from feeling insecure and vulnerable. Over time it became something which provided confidence, 'something I could rely on…that would never let me down'. Many other people say anger becomes their default position, the slot they keep falling back into because it's so familiar.

As children we all developed distinct personalities that help us cope with the fact that things don't always go our way. This is a natural part of human development. (You'll know from your own experience and other people's too that not only does life sometimes not go your way, it can be downright cruel at times, sometimes from a very early age.) Developing a personality and the attitudes and ways of thinking that go with it is a way of trying to

71

make sense of the world, of relating to it. As the disappointments and pain of life start to appear when we're small (as they inevitably do, for everyone), we start to react, each of us in different ways. Some people become withdrawn, others try to please other people. Still others try to control everything. Another strategy is to revel in the emotions. After a while, we tend to stick with one particular strategy. It becomes a habit.

Anger may have been part of your strategy for coping with life and the situations you found yourself in. It may have been a way of protecting yourself, a good strategy for that young person who was you, who knew nothing else. You used it (or some other strategy) as a way of shoring up your sense of self. That may have been all you knew, and it served its purpose, for a while.

But at some point, we all start to wake up to our habitual ways of being – like anger – and the fall-out, and realise we need to do something. We start to look for a way out.

There are lots of ways you can work with anger – reading books, talking with people, going on courses. Explore all of those if they are available and of interest to you. But know too that there is absolutely nothing like meditation for giving you a little room to manoeuvre around your emotions. Meditation can be the main tool you use to work with anger, to complement other available means.

When you start out, it's tempting to think that meditation will make your anger 'shut up'. Alan, who you'll hear from in the next few pages, certainly hoped this would be the case, and that he would never get angry again. But he learned to sit and be with it, instead of acting on it. He began to accept it instead of fighting it, and by looking deeply into it with stillness and curiosity, it began to transform.

I used to think that I was not 'good' at meditation – and that I was falling short in life – because I still got angry (and depressed and all of the other so-called negative emotions). In fact, these feelings are part of being alive and you don't need to try to escape them. Feeling angry does not mean you have failed or haven't quite 'got it' yet.

When you get angry, instead of thinking, 'Damn, I'm feeling cross, which is not what meditation or my life is supposed to be about. I'm getting this wrong!' keep looking with focus and curiosity at how it is, how you are as anger happens, whether you are in seated meditation or just going about your life. Don't wish it away, or try to push it away. By developing concentration and real interest, you can see it more clearly and relate to it more harmoniously. Stick right with it when it is strong and seemingly overpowering. Stay with your breathing, and see how anger changes and how much power it has to push you around.

It takes tenacity and patience to keep putting up with your own anger in this way. But many people inside have found that it does pay off and that, gradually, another way naturally unfolds. The friend who wrote that anger gave him confidence went on to say he learned to use meditation to calm himself down and regulate all the emotions that come:

> 'Emotions are a part of life... Meditation gives me the key to unlock the doors that have been welded shut for years due to my insecurities. Now I'm an open book: I can talk about my emotions and not feel judged... With the right tools, we can all have hope.'

Quite right!

Alan, HMP Kirklevington Grange

Note: This correspondence began while Alan was in HMP Lindholme; later he was moved to HMP Kirklevington Grange.

Hello Phoenix,

I am serving a six-and-a-half-year sentence for a crime of domestic violence brought on by years of drink and drug abuse. I did seek help outside, before my crime, but unfortunately my referral to anger management didn't arrive on time, and I ended up in here. I'm not passing the buck: I take full responsibility for my awful actions. A mate from prison was leaving to go home and handed me your yoga CD. I love it. I find the bending and stretching rewarding and the breathing exercises fantastic. But I find meditation hard.

The root of my anger lies inside me somewhere, and I believe that meditation will locate it and tell it to shut up. I am pleased with the changes I have gone through already, and I'm determined to work hard to keep changing. This is my first time in prison. I am 46 years old, and prison frightens the hell out of me. I would appreciate anything you can help me with.

Yours,
    Alan
....

Dear Alan,

Thanks very much for your letter.

It's totally normal to find meditation difficult – it's quite different from anything else we are taught to do or come across in daily life. The really important thing to understand is that meditation is not about achieving anything – not even a perfect calm state. Of course it's natural to want that, and I think if you keep practising yoga and meditation you'll sometimes find that lovely calm feeling of peace, but not always. Even for people who've been doing it for years, meditation is sometimes difficult and boring. But it's worth carrying on – I'll tell you why in a minute.

A 'good' meditation session, when you've 'achieved' meditation, is one in which you've kept bringing your attention back to the breath over and over, even if you haven't ended up feeling especially peaceful. I know it's frustrating when your mind keeps wandering off, and better when you're able to focus (I've got a very wandering mind!) but try not to judge yourself. The real point of meditation is to notice how thoughts and feelings are always coming up in our minds, including anger, worry and fear, and to learn to let go of them.

You'll find that practising yoga and meditation won't make your anger totally shut up, Alan. To be honest, you probably wouldn't be a complete human being if you never felt angry. What it *will* help you to do is to see how anger comes and goes (you probably can already), like clouds travelling across the sky, and how you don't need to let it control you. The ideal Alan won't end up being someone who goes around feeling peaceful all the time – but he'll be a man who can notice when he's starting to get annoyed, stop the anger growing, and choose not to do stupid or hurtful things out of anger – and perhaps then gives himself a pat on the back for dealing with those feelings, instead of giving himself a hard time. How does that sound?

Do you still have a problem with drink or drugs? If so, I hope you're getting help with that from a doctor or addictions team, but yoga and meditation can also help with this too, as it reduces stress and helps you to get out of bad habits. We can talk more about that if you want to.

Love and blessings,
    Rachel
....

Dear Rachel,

Security at Lindholme won't let me have the books you sent me. I have been told that I should be allowed them, but nothing seems to happen. I ask every day about the books. It's not like I am a bad prisoner: I don't have any IEP write-ups, or any conflicts with staff or inmates. I am so glad I do yoga and meditation because normally I would have snapped and been put down the block for five days as a result.

I also have visits mysteriously cancelled, mail going missing and in five months of being here they still will not give me any sort of employment. Anyway, all that has nothing to do with you. But in a way it has, because this proves that your CD works. Besides turning me into a 'rubber jointed man' able to move like a gymnast, it has done wonders for my temper. So, thanks! I am getting through my sentence so much easier now. I have found acceptance a lot easier through yoga and listening to the breath.

I loved your summer newsletter. The accounts of other inmates from round the country who have benefited from yoga helped me realise that we are not alone and can find peace through yoga and breathing.

Recently I read a book from the library which teaches about breathing and about the inner self. The ego is a separate entity to yourself, and once we realise this, the pain you carry goes away with the now-exposed ego.

Cheers Rachel,
   Alan

....

Dear Alan,

I'm sorry you aren't allowed to have the books we sent. You might find them in the library, or perhaps there's another inmate who could lend you one, or you could try asking a chaplain if they would get hold of the books. Having said that, I wouldn't be too bothered about having them if I were you. It sounds like you've already made a good start understanding how yoga and breathing exercises can help you, and I'm sending you some other things instead.

That book you mentioned sounds like it's helped you a lot. The only thing I would say about what you wrote about the ego is: be gentle with yourself! You're right that we need to let go of the ego's demands about how the world should be, and learn to accept what is, but remember that we all develop an ego to help us deal with the world. It's like having stabilisers on your bike when you're a kid. Not good to keep them on forever, but it usually takes a little while for a child to learn to manage without them, and it's best to be very encouraging and gentle with them while they learn. Same with our egos: we need to let go, but be kind to yourself (and others) while you learn. I've had to learn that (I'm still learning it!). Does that make sense?

I hope you carry on with the yoga and breathing exercises. It really does help even when things are tough. I had an accident on my bike a few days ago and woke up in hospital feeling very confused and not able to remember things properly. (I'm fine now.) But I remembered about breathing deeply and it did help me feel calmer and not start getting attached to the worrying thoughts going across my head. I just let them go.

Love and blessings,
Rachel

....

Hello Rachel,

Nothing much alters here in Lindholme – the books *still* haven't arrived! – but I find I am changing dramatically through using yoga and the breath. Old feelings like guilt, rage, hate and even jealousy seem to be dissolving. You were right about the mind, wanting to drift during meditation.

If it were up to me I would make meditation and yoga compulsory in schools and prisons. There would be a lot more level-headed people walking around. Before I came to prison, I couldn't draw a picture to save my life. Nowadays I am constantly drawing cartoon pictures of my grandchildren, and funny/silly foiled attempts to escape. So yoga can also bring about creativity. I love what it is doing to me.

Thanks,
Alan

....

Image by Alan

Dear Alan,

It's obviously frustrating for you, not to be able to receive the books. I don't know why you can't, and I don't think it's worth bothering about why things that are beyond our control happen. Often we can't find answers to those 'why?' questions, or we're not happy with the answers, so asking them just leads to anger and frustration. The really important question is, how are you going to respond? And you already seem to have realised that the best answer to that question is acceptance. All life – inside and outside prison – is full of situations we can't change, and when this is fully accepted things are a lot easier.

I'm reading an amazing book at the moment – the diaries and letters of Etty Hillesum, a young Dutch Jew who lived in Amsterdam during the Second World War. At the beginning of her diary, in 1941, most of what she writes is about falling in love, seeing her friends, her work, etc. Then gradually, she writes about all the restrictions that are put on the Jews having to wear a yellow star, not being allowed to go into greengrocers or into the houses of non-Jews (so she's not supposed to visit loads of her friends), they have to hand over their valuables to the Nazis, they're not allowed to cycle or use the trains anymore, so Etty gets blisters from having to walk long distances and she can no longer see her parents who live in the country. The amazing thing is that as she is allowed to do less and less, Etty's heart and soul become freer and freer. She says that even though there are so many places she can no longer go, the sky above her head is as big as it always was, and no-one can take that away. She says no-one can take away from her anything that really matters, unless she lets them. She doesn't allow the Nazis to stop her feeling that life is meaningful, or let hate take over her, so she carries on enjoying life. In the end she actually volunteered to go and work at a camp in eastern Holland from where thousands of Jews were sent to be gassed at Auschwitz. She didn't know that that's exactly what was happening to them, but everyone knew that Jews were being killed in Poland and the camp was full of suffering people who were very afraid of what would happen to them, and she wanted to be there to help people until it was her turn to be carted off to Poland. She was, in the end, and died at Auschwitz aged only 29, but she threw a postcard from the cattle truck she was transported in, which said, 'Tell them (her friends) we have left the camp singing.' I find her really inspiring.

I think if Etty were around now, what she'd say about your situation is that if you don't give in to anger about the books and other problems, if you stay calm and polite while trying to sort things out, then nothing has really been taken away from you – and in fact you'll have learned through practice most of what the books could teach you anyway!

It sounds from what you say that you're on the right track with your practice since you can already see how you're changing for the better as a result, so I'd say the best thing to do is carry on, trying to be more and more focused. You might want to spend more time doing the simple meditation, which is probably the hardest: sitting with your back straight, just counting the breaths and constantly bringing your attention back to that task when it wanders. I'm sure you'll find yourself advancing if you could do this every day for stretches of 20 minutes, half an hour, or longer.

Of course, the other important challenge is to take the practice more and more into your everyday life – being able to be more mindful of what you are doing and how you are being during all the ordinary things you do each day. You'll probably find this starts naturally if you're doing a lot of yoga and meditation practice, but you could help to develop this kind of mindfulness by putting in place little moments when you deliberately have a pause before you start eating, or focusing carefully on washing your hands and nothing else each time you wash them.

I hope you find this helpful – let me know what you reckon if you decide to try it. All the best and I hope you continue feeling calm.

Love and blessings,
  Rachel

....

Dear Rachel,

Things are moving along nicely. I am now working in the gardens, and loving it. On the out, I work in construction, as a steel fixer and concreter, so it is very physical. I thought after being idle for nine months, I would have stiffened up quite a lot and that working the gardens would have hurt like hell. Thank you yoga: I'm as fit as a fiddle and feeling no pain for my labouring.

Yours very calmly,
  Alan 'Freebird'

....

Hi Freebird!

I'm really glad to hear you're working in the gardens now. Even as we draw towards winter I hope you'll carry on enjoying these things. Working in a garden, you see things growing, doing well, dying away, then growing again. Lots of things changing, but at different rates and usually not everything dead at once – a bit like our lives!

I'm also glad that the yoga practice is keeping your body fit. How's the mind – is that keeping fit too? Are you finding you can focus during yoga and meditation at least sometimes? You might find that focus happening for short bursts at other times too.

Keep up the good work. Love and blessings,
Rachel

....

Hello Rachel,

Two women here, Vicky and Anna, were delighted about me doing yoga and said I should sit and think about how far I have come since coming to jail. I did this one night, during the week whilst listening to Radio 2 after a yoga session. Radio 2 then played a record so fitting it was as if I had been meant to hear that record. The skin over my body moved, quite ghostly actually, to 'Changes' by David Bowie. 'Turn and face the strain, ch, ch, ch, changes, come on all you rock and rollers.' This is the first time I have really sat and thought about my progress and the first time I feel I deserved a pat on my back. Sorry if this seems like the words of a man with a big head. These are the words of a very proud man and if I can come this far, so can anyone.

Take care,
Alan

....

Dear Alan,

Your letter didn't sound like you're a man with a big head – it is really good to celebrate the progress you have made. Someone else I write to said he was starting to like himself for the first time and I said that's great, because it's easier to help someone you like!

Are you still working in the gardens? You'll be seeing changes out there too – most things dying off. Perhaps things are dying off in you too, to make way for new growth? It sounds like it.

You'll need to look after the way you're growing - keep pulling the weeds out!

While you're going through this period of feeling strong and positive, it's a really good time to practise the meditation that can help you stay on track in the future even through rough patches. Meditation helps us see that things change all the time, and that a lot of our problems come from worrying about how things might be in the future, or trying to block things out through drugs etc. But if we can learn through meditation to just deal with one moment at a time we can cope with what life throws at us. Does this make sense?

Love and blessings,
    Rachel

....

Dear Rachel,

What a proper mess I'm in, Rachel. For over 12 months now, I have been drink and drug free, which I am extremely proud of. But I seem to be going backwards. No, I haven't given in and started drink or drugs. When I look around, I see what drugs are doing to other inmates and I feel truly repulsed at the thought of taking anything, ever again. Because of this, my terrible ego hates me with a passion and I am now suffering from bouts of fierce rage. Why is the ego so powerful? It does not live, so why can't I just switch it off? I knew I was going to have to face quite a bit of resistance, but not like this. I practise my yoga and my meditation and the ego hates it. Instead of it getting weaker, it seems to become stronger.

How the hell can I be rid of something that can even disguise itself as happiness? Every time I am doing well, it hits back at me. I am having terrible trouble sleeping. When I can't sleep I become furious and start cursing and blaming God for everything. I didn't know the battle was going to be this hard. At times I feel like giving in to it and I wish for my death. If I had the balls I would do it and then I would be rid of it. If I give in now, then I have wasted ten months of damned hard work. But how do I defeat such a powerful thing? How long does this battle go on for? When will it give up? Will I ever beat this horrible thing? One of us has to lose and I am prepared to keep fighting, but I am at my wits' end. I need to sleep properly but I will not ask for sleeping pills because that only leads to another addiction and it is false. Is there any yoga or meditation method that will knock me out at night time?

I am really sorry for sounding like I am going backwards. I don't want to give in to something evil which does not have a life force of its own. This is my life, not its.

I remain hopeful,
Alan

....

Dear Alan,

It's brilliant you're not giving in and turning back to drugs – this means you're definitely NOT going backwards! I've worked with users and managing to stay clean when you're under a lot of stress shows how strong you are and how far you've come. Also, if you're not venting your rages on others, only cursing God (who can take it), that's excellent as well, so keep up this great work and get as much help as you can with staying clean.

But I hear how you're feeling and it's tough. You can't get rid of your ego, Alan, and you can't beat it or your rage in a battle. But that doesn't mean it'll beat you, or that you can't do anything to help yourself – you can!

First thing is to understand that this whole idea of a battle and winners and losers is just that – just an idea. I'm not saying, 'You're a nutter, of course you can't hear your ego!' because when I've suffered from depression and anxiety I've heard that voice inside saying, 'You're pathetic and life is not worth living.' But through meditation I've learnt that this stuff comes from the mind, and that it's possible to let go of these stories the mind tells us, and no matter how impossible it seems, the stories and feelings don't go on forever. Even in this difficult time you'll probably notice that you're not feeling rage or despair all the time.

There are two things you can do to help. The first is to use yoga and meditation to help you accept these feelings as part of being human and sit with them without letting them take over you. That's not the same as trying to use yoga and meditation to get rid of the ego or feelings. That's the really hard part – to accept that meditation doesn't necessarily stop difficult feelings, you just start to be able to cope with them.

One time I was feeling so anxious that I threw up. But my parents were visiting me and I didn't want to worry them so when I came out of the bathroom I acted as if I was fine and suddenly understood the idea of 'standing behind a waterfall'. I could feel all these horrible feelings and fears rushing through my body like a waterfall. But they weren't carrying me away and drowning me because using breathing, I was standing behind the waterfall, able to carry on a conversation with my parents. You can 'stand behind the waterfall' of your rage, Alan, if when you practise, you just breathe and notice your anger, breathe and say, 'I'm feeling rage.' Breathe and stay in that place, close to the waterfall but not letting it sweep you away into all the other thoughts like, 'Why can't I get to sleep? I should be able to sleep, it's not fair. I've worked so hard, I'd be better off dead.' And if you do get swept away, then just as soon as you notice, remember you always have a life raft with you – your breath – so you just climb out by going back to the practice, breathing and noticing.

I find tree pose very helpful because you can't really balance and think at the same time. I suggest you try doing it opening your arms wide, breathing in deeply, opening yourself to love, peace and calm, but also opening yourself to accepting your feelings of anger so that they can just pass through and eventually out the other side – like shit to be honest! Doesn't stay inside forever!

Okay, that works, but it is hard. So I'll give you a second tool: you can change the story you're telling yourself about your ego. Instead of seeing it as a fighter getting stronger which is threatening to beat you, another way to see it is that in fact it's on its last legs and fighting desperately because it's afraid of your strength and of being killed off altogether (which wouldn't be good because we need a bit of ego). So then you could stop fighting and reach out to this poor old ego and say, 'Don't worry, I'm not going to finish you off, I've just been trying to change and I know it's frightening for you but it'll be okay.' I think you might find the battle disappears if you can do that, and the ego won't have 'won' or been destroyed. Remember that your ego is part of you, so as long as you fight it you are beating yourself up. There are times we need to be pretty tough, like when giving up drugs, but there are times to be gentle.

So how would it be, Alan, to go and do some yoga, and then sit quietly and tell yourself this new story: 'I've been doing really well. Part of me has been afraid of the changes I've achieved and it's natural to be afraid of change. I don't need to listen to these stories that are coming from my fearful mind any more. All I have to do is to let the good within me rise up and the rest will therefore wither away gradually. For the time being this may mean I carry on feeling rage and finding it hard to sleep but I'll accept that and I won't beat myself up any more.' Say to yourself, 'I'll look after you, Alan, because I love you and I know you are good,' and see how that feels, and then enter into meditation where you let go of *all* stories (the new story I've suggested is as real as the old battle one, and stronger, but in the end is just a story too), and just sit and be.

Love and blessings,
Rachel

....

Hello Rachel,

Discovering yoga is like escaping from hell. It is the key to the chains that we humans tend to shackle ourselves with and a beautiful way to God.

Since August 2011, my mother had been suffering from cancer. On New Year's Day, my mother was rushed into hospital for the last time. On the 5th I was taken from Lindholme to Huddersfield Royal Infirmary to say my last goodbyes. This was after the prison had forgotten to pass a message on to me in the morning that I had to get there as fast as possible. I was surprised at how calm I felt and even when I saw my mum, I remained calm. On the 7th my mum passed away, which I had to find out for myself because yet again messages were not passed on. I still remained calm. On Monday the 16th, it was my mother's funeral. Obviously a very big emotional day for the family. But we would be together and could help each other with cuddles, etc.

At 10 a.m. I was listening to Radio 2 and heard a traffic report saying that the M62 westbound was closed due to a big pile-up in the morning. This was the route we were going to be taking, so I went and told an officer about it, just to be on the safe side. At 11.45 a.m. we set off from Lindholme, and I asked if anybody had checked the road reports. I was told, 'It should be clear by now.' Nobody checked nothing. We headed down the M62, and caught up with the backlog of traffic after about ten miles. We sat in the queue of traffic for two hours and eventually turned back for the prison. Of course, I was devastated and terribly upset, but, somehow I remained calm and accepted it. Never in my life have I been so proud of myself. I know for a fact that the ego-driven person I used to be would have gone berserk and got me into a lot of trouble.

My mother would be, and probably is, so very proud, that her son has come this far. The lads in here and the officers are totally amazed at my serenity and, to be honest, so am I.

Rachel, I thank you from my heart. God bless,

Alan

....

Dear Alan,

What an amazing letter! I think you're right that your mother is proud of you. I also think – and I think you'll know this – that in one sense you didn't actually really miss what was really important about the funeral. If you'd gone berserk, like the old you might have done, then yes, you'd have missed it because you'd have been busy shouting and feeling angry and getting into trouble. No room there for feelings of love and thanks for your mum's life, no room to remember your family. Instead, by calmly accepting what happened, you were able to feel the grief and stay in the moment, and act in a way I'm sure was helpful to your family as well as impressive to the staff and inmates at HMP Lindholme. I'm sure your family missed you, and I'm very sorry for the loss of your mother and that you didn't make it to her funeral, but you have discovered an absolute treasure in your life and your mother's spirit lives on with you. The way you responded turned that day of the funeral from being what could have been a really terrible day in your life (and other people's) into a day you'll be able to look back on with pride and gratitude, and draw strength from in future when you have difficulties.

I hope it goes well when you move to Kirklevington. I'm sure you'll be a good example there!

Keep shining Freebird! Love,
   Rachel

....

Hello Rachel,

I hope and pray all is well with you. Well, here I am, I made it to the best Cat D prison in Britain. I thank God for this reward, and for loving and never giving up on me. There is a reading in the Bible, from James 1:2–5, that speaks of perseverance in the trials of life. As you can imagine there are times in prison when laying on your bed and drowning in self-pity seems like the only option.

I have found that it is exactly at times like this when perseverance becomes a living thing. I took great strength from reading the opening of *James*. It tells us that none of our long, hard work will ever be in vain. Throughout my sentence, Rachel, more and more of life's secrets keep opening up for me, making my journey a little easier. I thank you for teaching yoga to me and, with it, perseverance.

I am working on the gardens, with hope of eventually being trained in landscaping and green-keeping. The prison is running a golf course project in Middlesbrough at the moment and, boy-oh-boy, would I like to work on that. What about this, Rachel? On Monday night I have been asked to lead a meditation night for a handful of the lads, in the chapel. I am absolutely delighted.

My dad and brother were up to visit me yesterday. It is the first time we have seen each other since my mother passed away. It was a beautiful visit. All the hard work has been worth it.

Thank you and take care,
    Alan

....

Dear Alan,

You are so right about perseverance. That is one of the keys that has unlocked your prison door – your prison of anger and all the other negative stuff you were locked up in. You could be right that getting to HMP Kirklevington is a 'reward' for your perseverance. Personally I don't think it's a reward from God in the same way as you might give a child sweets for being good, because it suggests that if other people are suffering it must be because God thinks they don't deserve a reward, and I don't think that's true. But that's just my view.

What I think is, you've done such a lot of work that you've got to a place now where you can appreciate anything good around you, any opportunity you've been given. So you are pleased to be in Kirklevington, but my guess is that if you'd been sent to a different Cat D prison you'd have made the best of that and seized opportunities there too, instead of complaining. Being able to see the best of life, be grateful for things, and accept whatever is difficult – that's what you've learnt and that's your reward. And God is part of that because God is what you've opened yourself up to and got 'inside' with, since God is the source of joy, truth, love and beauty. Well, that's how I see it anyway, but if you see it differently that's fine – we all have different words for things and the important thing is that it's obvious perseverance has worked for you and you are now able to help yourself and others, being a channel for God's love.

Keep flying, Freebird!
Rachel

....

Hello Rachel,

I am now the OMU Orderly (a very trusted job), and have also been heavily involved with the gardens and a new build project within the ground. This has been a dream come true for me. Recently, I have also become the Induction Orderly as well. I love being busy.

I have no bad temper left, I have no vengeful thoughts. I have no yearning for drugs or alcohol, and I am able to leave the past where it belongs. My time in prison has been well spent. I have found great things within and new talents that I will use for the rest of my life. My new talents (including a huge amount of patience) and the way I now feel, can only be down to the finding of a beautiful thing called yoga. Without yoga, my sentence would have been as hard as some of the people's around me on a daily basis. I truly believe that without yoga, I would still be the very same angry, selfish, horrible being that I was three years ago.

Don't get me wrong, I do still have moments where my emotions almost get the better of me, then from absolutely nowhere, and totally unrehearsed, another voice kicks in and simmers me down almost instantly. I am so glad that I started this wonderful journey. It is a journey that does not stop when I leave prison in March. The prison sentence was simply a stepping stone into a better way of life. Without it, I wouldn't have found the beautiful peace of mind that resides within.

89

Thank you for all your love and support through probably the hardest times in my life. I thank God as well, for loving and never giving up on me.

Take care,
   Alan, The Freebird

....

Image by Alan

Frank, HMP The Mount

Dear PPT,

It's been a while since I wrote but I've been practising a lot. There was a time when anger felt like hot curry powder in my joints and flowing around my veins. It felt like I was poisoned, like my mind was destroying my body and in return my pain-infested body was destroying my mind. Standing up straight and relaxing my shoulders was impossible, it was too painful. My mind would torment and torture me from the exact nanosecond I woke up until late at night, lying in bed trying to sleep. Without heavy duty drugs, insomnia was a way of life.

Things seem so different now. I have learnt to relax and chill out and to observe and be conscious. I am learning that my mind is actually quite nuts and can affect my body in very negative ways. I have become aware of an 'observer'. This seeming separation of my mind and an observer was a key turning point. Now I know I don't have to buy into the madness of my mind, there is something behind it. I can't describe this something but whatever it is, I'm grateful it's there.

I do still find it hard to get in touch with my feelings sometimes. My gut tells me sadness is something I have a lot of. Today after my morning sitting I stopped and thought about myself and how I feel about myself. My awareness shot to the memory of me as a little boy, and I felt a cocktail of sadness, feeling sorry, and kindness or maybe compassion, for this little boy, who I realise is still within me.

Sometimes I feel a vast space down inside my body that is so still. Anger can come back like a tidal wave and if I'm quick I observe it and the flames die very quickly and I feel like I've grown or maybe changed. This is so empowering.

My friend and I were in the yard yesterday and he said, 'Be thankful for what we are learning, be thankful for being you.' I'm going to miss my friend when he goes out next week. He is going out with no licence after many years. I am excited for him.

91

Your friend,
Frank

....

Dear Frank,

I'm really glad you wrote. It was great to hear about the changes you're going through, and how you're relating to your feelings in a different way.

Anger and sadness are often closely related, like two sides of a coin. Losing something or someone you love, made to feel unwanted or inhuman – these things can make you deeply sad. But sometimes just being sad doesn't bring you any sense of control, of being able to affect things. Anger is an alternative way of re-establishing a sense of self, even if it continually puts you in conflict with those around you. Sometimes it attracts violence, but oddly enough, that can feel preferable to being ignored if you haven't yet found a way to really love yourself.

By starting to remember yourself as a little boy in that powerful and vivid way you described, you are really starting to get in touch with a sadness which you've probably been carrying around for a long time, unexpressed directly but coming out instead through anger. By recognising and allowing that sadness, you may start to see your relationship to anger changing for the better.

It was an appropriate and healing response you had, to be compassionate towards that younger you, though of course it was a spontaneous reaction for you, not you 'trying to be nice'. That aspect of yourself that cares for the hurt and the disadvantaged – that is you too!

That impossible-to-describe thing behind the 'madness of your mind' – one friend calls it the Holy Whatever – is what you need to keep opening yourself to, as you know how to do well by now, Frank, whether it is in seated meditation or when you are up and living your day. Hurray for everything you are discovering. Keep up the good fight!

With love,
  Sam

ANGRY

No sooner has it become silent
than I get angry.
I would not have thought
that I was so angry.
That I am still angry.

Angry with this or that person
who recently
or a long time ago
hurt
or betrayed me.

I sit in silence
and would like above all
to take vengeance.

Really?
I stay here.
And hear how the silence says:
that is how it was.

I stay here.
And hear how the silence says:
this is how you are.

I stay here
with the silence.

Sylvia Ostertag

Darren, HMP Wakefield

Darren has been in touch with the Prison Phoenix Trust since the 1990s. In 1996, he was put in solitary confinement and remained there for five years (in a cell known as The Cage). Six prison officers in riot gear were present each time the door opened, driving him back against the wall by a shield, which remained two inches from his face. He never saw another prisoner or anyone other than these officers. Over the years, Darren's situation changed, and his door could be opened with just three officers in ordinary uniform present.

Today, things have changed even further, as this exchange with Sandy shows, though Darren might quip that nothing has changed! He has been deeply committed to his tai chi and chi gong practice for many years, as well as meditation.

Dear Sandy,

You asked about how the change in my way of thinking has come about. I've never really thought about how the thoughts that used to plague and dominate my mind no longer do. In the past, they popped into mind so suddenly and so often that it seemed they were constantly there. Because I clung onto them when they came and fed them with endless different scenarios, they got stronger and it seemed like they were constant. It was like having a TV inside my head, stuck on one channel that I couldn't turn off. Even in sleep it was blaring away. It was very draining.

All this despite reading Buddhist teachings since I was 18: this was happening in my early thirties. It was like the Zen parable where a monk walking down a quiet lane sees a huge, black horse charging along with a man struggling to stay on. As the horse nears, the monk shouts: 'Hey, where are you going?' and the man, in desperation, shouts back: 'I don't know. Ask the horse!' That was like me. I knew and could see the horse but had no control of it.

The 'how' was just acceptance: I accepted I had all this anger and hatred, and violent thoughts that I didn't particularly want. But because I'd been thinking a certain way for so long (and at times deliberately so) it had developed its own habitual energy. These thoughts came whether I liked them or not and the more I tried to get rid of them, the more they resisted. There was a real battle for the mind, and because I desired a mind free of all that negativity, that very desire was adding to the conflict.

I expected my meditation to produce results and when it didn't, I got frustrated and angry, and lost more focus and the negativity grew even larger until it was monstrous.

In the end I simply stopped desiring. I still meditated, or tried to, but if anger came, it came. I didn't try to get rid of it. I just watched it. 'Okay, anger, you beat me. Do what you want, I won't resist any more. The mind is yours.' I expected nothing from my meditation. I just sat, and sat, and sat. Where in the past I had used methods, breathing techniques etc., this time I used nothing.

Whatever came into my mind I just watched, no matter what it was, I didn't judge it, didn't compare it, didn't label it. And over time, I realised 'like' and 'dislike' were relinquishing control of my mind. I no longer had preference of what I'd rather have in my head because whatever entered my head didn't seem to stay long enough to take root for either like or dislike to develop.

Like everyone ignorant of the internal processes, causes and conditions, I had looked externally for the cause of my problems. But once you're able to see the ceaseless internal reactions to the external stimulation, which result in emotional disturbances of every kind, you see the pattern of it all. Then it dawns on you that it doesn't have to be this way.

I still get angry at times, but it's like a flash. There is anger and there is *ANGER*. Everyone has experienced anger at some stage. It comes, stays momentarily, then goes and everything returns to normal. But *ANGER* is long term. It eats into your soul and becomes your norm, eventually poisoning you. Because my mind is relatively anger-free these days, I can see anger coming, feel it forming so I am able to stop it taking root. It's not the power it once was. It comes and goes so quickly because there's very little like or dislike to reinforce it. These days, no expectations. I suspect that if I wasn't able to see this internal process clearly, the construction of the 'I' and so on, the radical change I eventually made from one extreme to the other wouldn't have been possible.

When I was at my worst I was full of violent, conflicting thoughts nearly every moment of the day. I decided it's either all or nothing. I chose nothing. I wanted rid of everything, 30 years of worldly conditioning.

It's no good saying, 'Okay, I'll get rid of some thoughts but not all of them. I want to keep certain ones because they are so much a part of me.' If you want to get to the roots of the problem and dig them up so they cannot root any more, then all thoughts must go. You must experience that still, silent, thoughtless mind. The beauty of it now, ten years plus down the road of just sitting in silence, is that when I feel a thought forming, I can feel its energy ripples stirring the still surface of my mind. Thoughts don't disturb the inner depth. They're just surface ripples that come and go and there is nothing for them to latch onto. So they float by.

I wouldn't swap what I have re-discovered for anything in the world. Once you're mentally free, it doesn't matter where you may find yourself physically. It really doesn't.

Take care. Be happy,
  Darren

....

Dear Darren,

Somehow you have managed to articulate amazingly clearly how a truly life-changing decade has led to the quiet confidence and sense of freedom you show today. The courage it must have taken is breath-taking, and so is the account of your dedicated daily meditation. Thank you dear Darren for your honesty which showed me your step by step journey out of the misery of hatred and violent thoughts into a place of calm.

You show so well how meditation helped you see that when all-consuming violent thoughts besiege you, it is totally draining. And the more you try to stop negative thoughts, the stronger they become.

As you say, when you expect something from meditation, or try to attain something, it doesn't happen. 'We' are getting in the way. When the ego-led meditator wants a result, thinking that something can be achieved just by sitting, there is usually just disappointment and frustration. But as soon as you decided to give up fighting the thoughts, even the thought that just by meditating you'd get results, you were able to accept what was and what is without judgement.

When you stopped resisting, and said to anger, 'Okay anger, you beat me. Do what you want, I won't resist any more,' and just watched the angry thoughts as they swirled around, you gradually started to see through them. What you describe is a torment of thoughts that were out of control and all-powerful. Then when you were able to see that these thoughts and yourself were locked in a battle for supremacy and they were winning, you let go. Let go completely, even of thought itself! Except you were still drawn to sit and sit and sit in truly dedicated meditation practice.

Over this long period of time you became aware of how thought waves arise and dissolve in the mind and once you could see these waves you were able to stop labelling and comparing them. Best of all, you saw that it isn't just your external life that was the cause of your problems but what was compounding them was what was happening internally in how you reacted. When you can see the pattern, as you call it, then you can see that not only thoughts but states of mind too are waves arising and dissolving all the time from the mysterious depths of our being.

Then it dawned on you it doesn't have to be this way!

The sheer authority of that sentence blew me away.

You say that because you felt so full of conflict and violence after 30 years of conditioning, you wanted to rid yourself of everything, even of thought itself. And through dedicated sitting day after day, you were able to allow the wheels of the mind to rest. That was a wonderful manifestation of letting go and allowing. What a blessing...

In a sense, we cannot get rid of thoughts because as human beings we are programmed to think and probably if we didn't think at all, we'd need the doctor. But meditation is extraordinary in that when you let go, you wake up to something fully alive which is so much bigger than the small self which preoccupies us with its suffering. And the compassion of the universe from which none of us is separated touches us – and heals us.

It takes time. Ten long years of sitting every day for long hours for you. It doesn't matter where you find yourself physically now, you say – it really doesn't – because you are mentally free. I salute you in deep gratitude for your letter with my whole heart.

With love,
Sandy

....

Dear Sandy,

As you can see, I've been moved. The regime is similar to Wakefield, mostly bang-up, out of my cell for one hour exercise, one hour cardiovascular room and shower. But most days I've had well over one hour exercise. Some days two to three hours. I've been going out and they've been leaving me out there. I've been out in the sun for the first time in over 11 years. I never once saw the sun at Wakefield. There's a patch of grass outside my window. I see birds like pigeons and crows, and the first grass I've seen in over a decade.

I'm aware that we are but a part of something far greater. That we, the 'I', are not the centre of everything we see, the knower, the experiencer of it all. The owner, controller and if we wish the destroyer too. Tai chi and yoga and meditation open our eyes and minds to something greater than ourselves I suppose. It grounds us in the knowledge that we are one with everything. That there is no inner or outer, higher or lower.

For the past 500 days now, I've been doing something called muscle/tendon changing and marrow brain washing chi gong. It's very difficult. You're basically standing in and holding stress positions. It generates so much heat it's unbelievable. The pain or the constant ache that penetrates deep into the bones is intense. But it's a pain and ache that you get used to, even welcome, because of the power, the alchemical process that it activates within your body. If you can find that centre of calm, that pool of stillness while in a stress position and maintain it, then you can find that calm and stillness in any situation, and the reward of being able to do so is power which develops spirit, along with good health and a host of additional benefits.

Take care. Be happy. Hope all goes well with you.
　　Darren

....

Dear Darren,

Good to hear from you in a new location. Great that you are able to be in the sun. As you say, we are but part of something much greater and the 'I' is not the centre of everything we see. This one-with-everything you mention is a way of life, isn't it? One forgets it one moment and remembers another.

Being a pain-averse human being, may I ask if the exercise you've been doing for the last 500 days is the best way you feel you can find calm and stillness in any situation? Maybe the pain you talk of is no different than the challenge of long hours of Zen sitting on long retreats – I can identify with that. But people are always asking me about whether they should feel pain in yoga or meditation practice and although mental pain to some extent is unavoidable as the washing of our conditioning goes on, I shrink these days from inflicting pain on this miraculous body. More and more I have such sympathy with it – mine, yours, theirs, same thing.

So happy about the sun, grass, pigeons, crows, your wonderful physical ability. A lot to rejoice about.

With love,
Sandy

....

Dear Sandy,

Thank you for my letter. I am now on B-wing where I am out of my cell more for longer with three other prisoners. I still do my tai chi on the exercise yard first thing in the morning.

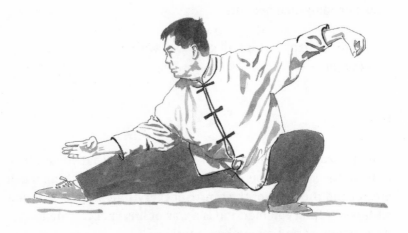

What I've noticed about being allowed out of my cell more to 'associate' and mix with others is that association is boring, more boring than being locked in your cell with nothing to do. Why is that? Is it because you're more aware of boredom – same old conversations with others, same old activities? Jumping from one to the other to try and hide from the reality – that all activities are boring once the novelty wears off. It's easier doing nothing, wanting nothing. It doesn't make any difference to me either way. I laugh at boredom. It creases me up when I see how bored other people are but do not know how to deal with it. Boredom is the elixir of life. It is also a poison. But if you know how to drink it, it will create new life. But you have to drink so much of the stuff that you almost choke on it. You have to be on that point of giving up, the point of death, before you start to see what lay beyond it.

I remember something Dzogchen wrote: 'If you were to fall to your death from a very great height, it would be a shame not to admire the view as you fell, or appreciate the wind in your hair or warmth of the sun in your face. To appreciate this raw voltage of being alive requires that we learn to lick honey from the razor's edge.' Familiarising oneself with boredom is walking the razor's edge. If you don't run and hide from it, behind the 10,000 distractions, you'll find the honey of life eventually. (Yum yum!) So I say boredom is the elixir – not just boredom, but all things we don't like or try to run from. Stick with them long enough. If they don't drive you insane, they'll become your robes, your alms bowl, your bread and butter of practice.

Thanks for the letter and the postcard. Take care. Be happy,
Darren

....

Dear Darren,

You say that association with others is more boring than solitude. If you want to try an experiment with that in conversation, try listening. Hardly saying a word, simply listening to what the other is saying and occasionally interjecting a question. People are actually quite interesting when they finally perceive they are genuinely being listened to and feel able to share things from their heart. It takes most of us a lot of trust.

When companions – whether you choose them or not – begin to speak from their core, it is hard not to listen to their truth because it frequently chimes with our own, strange as it may sound.

Not the same language and not the same understanding, nevertheless you might be able to discern an echo.

That's a fine quote about falling from a great height. Isn't this nothing other than listening to companions talking, doing tai chi in the morning, laughing, feeling bored? And walking the razor's edge and tasting the honey: isn't that what meditation is about? Isn't this the Way?

With you every single minute,
Sandy

....

Dear Sandy,

You ask what I would say to someone at Woodhill about to come here to Whitemoor. Well, if they were worried, I suppose I would tell them not to dwell on it, to stop thinking about what it might be like, because it is the thinking process that generates and maintains the worry/anxiety, etc. It sounds so simple, I know, and lots of prisoners have told me it's not easy. But I was once where they were, unable to switch off the thinking process. I know it's not easy. But there is no other advice to give. If it's too long-winded and complicated it will just confuse things and probably generate frustration to fuel more negative thinking. Because I can switch off the thinking process, I can only teach by example. Lads often say to me, 'I don't know how you done it/do it.' And I just say, 'I don't think about it. I have no preferences, no likes or dislikes, and I strive not to judge and compare this with that. My entire life revolves around the practice of non-attachment, even to the practice of non-attachment.'

People either get it or they don't. I don't do emotion. It's a waste of energy, it's mentally and physically draining, and yet it seems like everyone around me is drowning in a sea of it at times.

Be happy,
Darren

....

Dear Darren,

Welcome to Whitemoor and the chance to get out of the cell a bit more. That's good news.

You said that the thinking process generates and maintains worry, etc., and if you dwell on things you might get anxious. How right you are. But the problem is that we are programmed to think. It is the difference between being human beings and nearly all animals. It is a tremendous gift and because of the gift of thinking, we wear clothes, have tea to drink and food to eat, have shelter and medicine and technology and so on. But you imply that thinking and emotional states are intertwined and that is certainly often the case. So if you see a beautiful tree or smell fresh air, you can feel joy. I was sitting in an old church last night (rather an unusual visit for me) and in the dark night suddenly the bells rang out the time, catching me by surprise. It was a little hairs-on-the-back-of-the-neck moment for which I am grateful.

But being able to switch off thinking in meditation is a great boon, a refreshment to the mind and spirit and a way to live life off the cushion, unafraid to live fully, just as it arrives, knowing that fundamentally we are at one unseparated peace. You say you don't do emotion because it's a waste of energy and mentally and physically draining. I get that. I cannot imagine what strategies a person needs for staying calm in prison and often feel truly humbled by the things you write. If emotions sweep up, though, does it really matter at times? You know by now they are just waves of the mind and in this constantly changing THIS-NESS will dissolve again when they are ready?

Take care of yourself, Darren, and warmest wishes for your tai chi practice and your sitting. May both be full of peace, freedom and happiness.

Sandy

....

Dear Sandy,

As you can see from the return address, I'm no longer at Whitemoor. For a while I thought I might be going on normal location, but they were reluctant to put me straight out on to the wings after so long in solitary and only mixing in small groups of no more than eight since leaving the cages at Wakefield. They thought if anything were to go wrong, there wouldn't be the same level of supporting network as there is in here on the PIPE unit at Frankland. There's 19 lads on here. It was a bit strange at first, routine is less structured to what I've been used to the past 18 years. I don't even think less structured is the right phrase. It just felt different. The unit is bigger so maybe it was just the exposure to more space and I couldn't quite get my bearings. I'm kind of settled into a routine now. Been here nearly four weeks now. The exercise yard is much bigger and I can see the sky, without seeing it through the wire of a caged roof, for the first time in 18 years. And I get exercise on an evening, in the dark, which was a novel experience for me. Every opportunity I get to be outside in the fresh air, I'd rather be outdoors than indoors. I've spent 23 hours of every day of the past 16 years behind my door unable to get out in the fresh air so I suppose I appreciate being in the fresh air a bit more than others.

I get to go down the main jail once a week for the Buddhist chaplaincy, and when I start working if I choose the workshops I'll be mixing with the main jail, and I get the yard with the other three wings on Westgate Unit. So I am mixing with a much larger group of people. Slowly normalising me!

Anyway, take care. Be happy.
    Darren

....

Dear Darren,

What great news to hear that you have been moved to a unit at Frankland which has much more space but gradually that is beginning to seem okay. Thank goodness you can see the sky without a wire in the way and can even get outside for exercise at night. You say you'd rather be outside than inside despite the cold, and how I understand that. Sixteen years of 23 hours a day, unable to be in the fresh air. It brought me up short. No wonder you appreciate it so much. Thank goodness that terrible deprivation is behind you now.

It's good to hear you get down to see the Buddhist chaplain each week and that work is on offer if you choose to do it. Must seem very strange to have the prospect of mixing with the main jail while being with the other three wings on Westgate at the moment. Perhaps the Buddha's wisdom about this very moment, staying in this very moment, helps. What a lot of changes you are going through day by day, allowing yourself to acclimatise in your own space and time and relaxing with a little quiet time outside at night to restore and reset the system as it were. Sounds just right.

May all the light and infinite possibility of Christmas be with you,
   Sandy

....

When Darren next sent the PPT some artwork, he included a note:

Christmas on normal location, my first Christmas for 18–19 years. It went off okay. Just normal really, nothing spectacular happened. Went out on the exercise yard as usual and I done my tai chi. Then walked around, which I do every day anyway. I meditated in my cell and done my chi gong in the evening.

I was invited back up to the PIPE unit here on the morning of 21st December along with seven other lads who had recently progressed off PIPE, for a coffee morning. They had put on a little spread, baked x-mas cake, tea loaf cake, biscuits, etc. It was alright, something different that I'd never heard of or encountered before in prison. I had only left the PIPE unit a few weeks before, so it felt like I had never left.

All the best to you all for the new year. Take care, be happy,
   Darren

....

Hope

Believing that things are going to be okay – or just believing that *you yourself* are okay – is not easy in prison. So many things about prison can make it easy for you to feel hopeless. But many people manage to find hope, which gives them energy to carry on, even if it's hard at times. Ironically, it is by training their minds and hearts to be in the present that so many people say they find hope for what lies ahead.

Charlotte in Eastwood Park wrote that she found hope by turning a negative into something constructive. In her isolated situation, she said she couldn't get caught up in external distractions, so she began meditating and reading more, making peace with silence and feeling calmer.

Antonio writes about reframing a negative into a positive, turning a cruel bureaucratic decision into a source of joy. He found hope – not by blindly believing that the decision would somehow be overturned, but hope in himself, and in the human potential to flourish even under terrible conditions. He was able to do this thanks to the meditation and self-discovery he'd done in the previous months. Similarly, Hans finds himself thriving even in an unbelievably crowded and restricted prison in Thailand.

Hope doesn't arise randomly in Hans and the others who share their stories here. It emerges because they regularly spend time allowing their minds to become still and focused in meditation.

With practice, the part of your mind that you are familiar with – the active, thinking mind – is allowed to rest, and another part of your mind comes forward. That mind is naturally bright and radiant, like the sun, and it's begging to break through the clouds of your mind. Worry, fear, habitual thinking, planning, analysing, fantasising – these are the clouds that meditation helps dissolve. The thinking, controlling mind will start to slow down; this is the cloud cover getting lighter. As the sun gets stronger, you start seeing possibilities instead of dead ends. You notice beauty where previously all was grey. Where nothing had seemed worth your attention before, you are open to being awed.

On one hand, it doesn't make sense that you could ever feel hopeful when your situation is so bleak or unbearable. But things do start looking up as you develop the habit of focusing your attention – for at least a short while each day – on something other than all the mental activity related to your situation. Each time you sit down to meditate, you are inviting hope in. It's here already actually, clouds or no clouds.

Joe, Bristol Prison

The instruction in the yoga classes here on C-wing has been the most informative and educational experience I have ever had. After the class the other day, all nine of us sat together and spoke freely with hope, awe, good spirit and agreement. I've never seen nine people agree on anything, especially in the nick. It was extremely empowering and I witnessed deep change in all present. Our teacher's instruction is non-patronising, true, straight and spot on. It would be amazing if this was taught in schools or inner city estates as it is universally applicable to us all. Absolutely incredible.

I've been in trouble with police and authority since adolescence, from petty crime to robbery, following previous generations and peer groups in my area. Our yoga teacher is better than any judge, probation officer, teacher, police, lecturer or punishment giver. I felt genuine shame and remorse.

No-hopers only change when they can actually hear what they know is straight, true, achievable and gives reward in prisons. I have only known one truth – all inmates and repeat offenders who want to break the cycle are between a rock and a hard place. Self-pity, laziness, self-centredness is a trap we all fall into. We all dress it up a bit differently but it is just that. Everyone needs something to help overcome this and as meditation and yoga are put over, there is reward, self-responsibility and hope that we are able to break that cycle.

Graham, HMP Edinburgh

Dear Ava,

Thank you so much for your wonderful letter. It arrived just in time, as I'm floundering a bit with life here. There's an undercurrent of brutality, bullying and intimidation; there's a clique of drug users, their suppliers and hangers-on that seem to keep to themselves mostly, but one thing I can't fail to notice is a constant watchfulness and wariness among most of the cons.

A lot of big, brutal-looking bruisers just staring, barging in front at queues, helping themselves to the loaves and rolls supplied for all our breakfasts; constantly pushing, intimidating and creating an atmosphere of quiet desperation. Most faces are hard masks of machismo posing, like the posturing in a million playgrounds. I think part of the problem is mixing up older and younger prisoners, violent offenders with chronic drug addicts. There doesn't seem to be any logic to it. I have had deep feelings of fear, isolation and paranoia that I've managed to chase away by concentrating on the fact that they don't exist, while breathing in goodness and breathing out poison. But some days I can't shift an all-enveloping feeling of hopelessness. Sounds like I'm going backwards doesn't it?

I know that hell is on earth and hell is being led by the nose like a dumb animal, by your mind and emotions, from high to low and low to high in a matter of minutes, no peace at all, no comfort, no love. 'The path of yoga is not easy: every inch of ground has to be won against much resistance. The aspirant must be patient and firm to face all difficulties, and obstacles of all sorts with a calm and serene spirt,' as it says in *Becoming Free through Meditation and Yoga*. As much as I smile, say 'please' and 'thank you', and try to be pleasant to everyone, I'm met with mistrust and sometimes outright hostility which I do have to fight hard against – I would willingly wallow in fantasies of extreme vengeful violence as I once did, but that's just regressing to their level.

After being moved, I was beguiled by the demon TV for a while. After nearly three weeks of quiet solitude, my practising was regular and as my last letter probably shows, I felt myself in a state of grace. But I let it slip. Only four or five days in all, but after such a short time I undid so much good work, and now I'm feeling as though I'm starting from scratch. But I suppose I kept falling off my bicycle once the stabilisers were taken off, hey? So I'm forcing myself to get up early and practise meditation and yoga to fully charge mind and body for the day's battles. I've become quiet and choose solitude, though I do have a few good people I talk with, even just to smile and say 'Hi' nine times out of ten and have a conversation with, once in a while. But it is hard.

With love,
> *Graham*

....

Dear Graham,

You are so courageous in how you try to confront what you see going on around you.

Of course, sometimes the centredness fails and you can't stay aware enough to know that the emotions aren't you. You might intellectually reason and know how you *should* respond, but that doesn't help when the emotions take over.

I find this very hard myself at times. But this is where regular meditation practice comes in so that we get some 'ballast' in our ship which lurches from side to side in a storm (or even a light breeze occasionally!).

You say you must try harder, but if possible, just accepting your unacceptance can have the same result. You know, Graham, we live in *such* a punitive society and are so conditioned in our childhood to be *good* that I guess 99.9 per cent of us carry around a load of totally unnecessary guilt. Watching TV for a while is okay.

You are a pleasure to write to. You've made massive progress.

With love,
    Ava

....

Hans, Bombat Phiset Prison, Thailand

Hans has consistently been full of hope and joy from his yoga and meditation practice, helping him thrive in some difficult physical conditions in a Thai prison. He raises an issue that comes up for many people who take anti-depressants: he wants to stop taking them as the effects from his meditation and yoga become stronger. He does the right thing, following Caroline's advice to talk to medical staff. What she and other letter writers will also say to people in the same boat is: you are not a failure because you are on anti-depressants. Sometimes they are a useful tool. And finally, if you decide after talking with your doctor that you'd like to reduce them, make sure you do it gradually.

Dear Sir,

I am serving a 13-year sentence here at the Bombat Phiset Prison in Bangkok. I started doing yoga and meditation about a month ago, every morning at 5:30 a.m. It truly is working and I am so much more peaceful and self-loving than before. I still have moments with bad thoughts but far less than before.

I've been on Prozac for about a year. It's an anti-depressive medicine and the dosage is 40mg daily (not high). I have read that meditation helps. That's one reason I have started. Another reason is that I often think very negatively about people, and every time I notice it, I don't like it. My social worker friend is suggesting that I should not stop taking medication, as my current environment is not easy and I could fall into deep depression again. I must admit that medication is helping me, but I feel great changes since doing yoga and meditation. Could you advise me?

Sincerely,
Hans

....

Dear Hans,

You are so right when you say that yoga and meditation help depression. You are beginning to discover the benefits now you have started practising. While it may be desirable to try to reduce your anti-depressants, you need advice from a doctor. Coming off anti-depressants needs to be done gradually, over a long period.

Meanwhile, yoga and meditation are excellent alternatives, and many prisoners reduce their dependency on drugs through this. We recommend you keep up a regular daily practice, and it would be a good long-term goal to eliminate your medication – slowly but surely!

As you meditate, thoughts will probably arise in your mind, and tempt you to follow them. This happens to us all, and it takes discipline to return to the breath counting again. You can do it. Do not be concerned about the thoughts, even if they seem important. Just let them go, and return to counting your breaths again.

There may be plenty of noise around you and maybe even people in your cell but you can find a way to do it. First thing in the morning, or last thing before bed, are good times to practise. Try to practise at the same time every day so you develop a routine – whether you are happy or depressed, calm or gripped by too many thoughts, whether you feel well or ill.

Go well, go gently. Peace be with you,
  Caroline

....

Dear Caroline,

Thank you for the newsletter. I have read all of it already and now there are others reading it. Inmates from India and Nepal, and one guy from Nigeria. You have infected us all and we are crazy about yoga and meditation. As we are 52 in one cell, I start when all are asleep, at 5 a.m.

Thanks for your advice about my medication. Right now we have no doctors here. The people at the medical station are not real doctors. So I will continue with medication until I find professional advice.

It's very hot and we've been three days without water. Only two litre-and-a-half bottles for each person, for showering and drinking. I've got some drinking water hidden but most of the others don't. It's crazy, but I've got used to a lot in the three years I've been here. Meditation is really putting a smile on my face and gives me great peace. I'm a better man now and full of motivation. It's crazy. And I love it.

Thank you for the yoga handouts. I have given out a few and I'm sending one today to one pen pal from Nigeria. The problem with her is that she thinks yoga and meditation have something to do with worshipping and she is a hard-headed Christian. I've been writing to her a lot and sending info, but somehow I feel like I can't reach her.

Sending you love and peace,
  Hans

....

Dear Hans,

Your pen friend in Nigeria is not alone in thinking meditation does not mix with Christianity. All I can say is that meditation is primarily about clearing the mind of one's thoughts (and ultimately the ego). In doing this, many Christians find that meditation deepens their faith. One of the previous Directors of the Prison Phoenix Trust was Sister Elaine MacInnes, a Catholic nun, and she was a firm advocate of this style of meditation, to understate it massively! The quote from the Bible, 'Be still and know that I am God,' is often used by Christians who meditate. And we know that Jesus withdrew many times to the desert or quiet places. I don't know whether any of this is appropriate for your pen friend. Meditation is not everyone's way. It may be better just to accept that her way of Christianity is her way.

Go well, go gently. With all best wishes,
  Caroline

....

Dear Caroline,

Everything you send me is very precious and is attracting more and more people. The last seven days I have been lazy getting out of bed and missed my practice. This morning I started again and felt the kick of peace, calmness and joy during the whole day! Now I can't wait for the morning again. We are now 49 in one cell. You can imagine the noise. But it's worth waking up early.

I've been trying to do walking meditation but so far with no success as my breathing and mind gets completely messed up, and I don't find any results happening. I have the possibility once we get out of the room to do walking for about 20 minutes without being disturbed. Is it that walking meditation is harder to learn? Or am I doing it wrong?

Love and peace,
Hans

....

Dear Hans,

You have discovered what a difference it makes to the day when you meditate, compared to the days when you do not meditate. Wonderful.

As for walking meditation, I could describe the walking meditation practice I do, and which is used in Zen. Sit first for 25 minutes, then do walking meditation for five minutes, and then 25 minutes of sitting again, and so on. When you walk, hold your hands together when you rise to walk, left hand held in right hand facing upwards, at waist or stomach level. This will help stop thoughts being scattered. Try and have the same state of mind as sitting, keeping your eyes lowered, walking slowly, taking small even steps in a steady pace.

In addition to walking meditation, have you tried meditating when you do daily things, such as when you eat or drink?

We light a candle daily here in the office for people in prison, including you. May your light shine,
Caroline

···

Dear Caroline,

I've been doing my practice almost daily lately, and have inspired my friend who sleeps beside me, so we now share our place early at 5 a.m. and do yoga, pranayama and meditation together. It gives me more space and it's a lot easier. Thank you Caroline, you are one precious diamond.

All my love and light,
Hans

···

Dear Hans,

It is good you are practising with a fellow inmate. The more you can support each other, the more your practice will be sustained. The key is to keep to a regular daily practice, so keep going! I am so impressed given your difficult and crowded circumstances.

I also 'sit' in silence at the start of the day, but not as early as you! I am greatly helped in my practice by being part of a meditation group, and also by being with the Prison Phoenix Trust. There are times I read meditation books or poetry; there are other times when I just concentrate on the practice.

You continue to be in our thoughts. Go well, go gently,
Caroline

···

Dear Caroline,

I am a believer in the spirit and the instinct to follow the good like the love of God. The future will teach all people to stop hating one another because of religion, believing more in love and forgiveness. My practice is going great and today I see clear results: I avoided a fight and brought peace, even laughter, into a situation that months ago would have ended in a serious scrap. Like you said, it is important to keep on doing my daily programme and the results are there.

Lately, I have been doing a martial art called Muay Thai (kick boxing) and I have found my mind wandering now when I do meditation, so I'm thinking of stopping Muay Thai as I believe it is creating too much ego! I've been winning a couple of fights too, but I am not sure if it does me any good being all proud about myself. What do you think?

May the peace and blessings from Allah be upon you. (I'm reading the story of Prophet Muhammed, that's why I use Allah today.)

Te mando mi luz, amiga mia para siempre,[1]
   Hans

....

Dear Hans,

You made a profound comment about the need for love and forgiveness in this world, to transcend all religions. I think all true religions are about love and forgiveness at their core. The problem is when religion becomes the vehicle for dogmas and prejudices and intolerance.

Your observations that the kick boxing is having a detrimental effect on your meditation is real progress, and very perceptive. There probably is a way to fight and not let the ego be attached to winning, but maybe only when there is a need to fight, like in self-defence and not when picking a fight, and not when it is a want. However, I suspect it is very hard to achieve being able to fight without arousing the ego.

---

1   Spanish for 'I send you my light, my friend forever.'

Since you are reading the story of the Prophet Muhammed, I thought you would like the enclosed extract from Rumi. As you probably know, he is the 13th-century Persian scholar, theologian, poet, and Sufi mystic, whose works transcend national and religious borders.

Peace be with you,
Caroline

--- ∞ ---

Be empty of worrying.
Think of who created thought!
Why do you stay in prison
when the door is so wide open?
Move outside the tangle of fear-thinking.
Live in silence.
Flow down and down in always
widening rings of being.

Mewlana Jalaluddin Rumi,
13th-century Sufi mystic

--- ∞ ---

Dear Caroline,

Thanks for the poem from the Muslim. I really love it. I've got a lot of respect for the old Arab theologians, especially from Persia.

I have reduced my medication from about two months ago, and I feel absolutely fine. When I had to stop practising recently because of some back pain, I felt a bit strange, but now that I'm doing my morning practice again regularly, I feel great. Even my meditation seems to have improved after the break. I am going much deeper now and have barely any mind wandering. Stopping medication completely is my next goal.

Love and light,
Hans

Dear Hans,

It is great you have reduced your medication and also returned to your daily meditation practice. How interesting you notice your practice seems to have improved, and that you are going deeper. Sometimes this happens after a break. Perhaps it is about realising how much a meditation practice underpins your life, and you particularly notice it after a break. Whatever the reasons, keep on with your daily practice. As you say, it helps build up your confidence, and it will certainly help you when you transfer to Germany, and beyond that too!

Peace,
   Caroline

....

Dear Caroline,

Even if the prison here is getting worse, they can't change my good mood. The new rule is only three blankets per person. One for the floor, one to cover ourselves and one to use as a pillow. We are also not allowed to bring soap and toothbrushes into the cell. Today they have taken away all our clothes and they are allowing us only two shorts and two shirts. It is amazing what is happening, but still I take it with a smile. There are probably worse places than here and people suffering more than me. I pray for all to keep their strength up and keep their spirit shining. Can't wait to wake up in the morning! Now we are 50 in one cell and often it's not easy, but still I get my few moments of absolute peace. It's like a personal treasure.

Love,
   Hans

....

Dear Caroline,

They keep issuing harder rules. A couple of weeks ago we had to throw away all our belongings like clothes, books and anything that doesn't fit into a small locker. They want to harden the lives of prisoners so that people don't come back to prison any more. I don't think it's going to work, but if instead they considered better education and teaching other life opportunities, they might be able to change people's attitudes.

My practice is still going well. I wake up at 5 a.m., and do yoga until 5.40, then there is a Buddhist prayer relayed over the speakers in the jail for half an hour, and during that time I do pranayama and meditate. It is not easy, because there is always somebody going to the toilet or looking for cigarettes. It can still disturb me but I take it much easier than a year ago. And sometimes I catch this moment during meditation that takes me away and fills my soul with peace. Even if it's only a few seconds out of 30 minutes' meditation, I feel this love surrounding me the whole morning. I welcome the day so much better now and have decided that for the coming week, I will stop medication.

Exercise: Hold it Right There!

Hans mentions *pranayama* several times. This word is sometimes translated as 'breathing practice' or 'breath control'. But you may like to come up with your own translation, as you discover something powerful and peace-giving that is about far more than just holding and counting the breath. This is what you do:

1. Sit in one of the positions described in the first part of the book, so that your back is straight and your chest is open. You can close your eyes, if that's comfortable. Now soften the body around the upright spine. Let go of any tension in the jaw, the hands, the shoulders, the small of the back and the belly.

2. Breathe in for a count of 5. Each count can be a second long, or you can use your heartbeat to help you count.

3. Now hold the breath for a count of 8. Don't hold the breath if you have untreated high blood pressure or glaucoma. And don't hold the breath up to 8 if it feels uncomfortable.

4. Then breathe a slow out-breath, for a count of 8.

5. At the end of the out-breath, let the body be empty of breath for a count of 5.

6. Repeat:

Breathing in	5
Holding breath	8
Breathing out	8
No breath	5

Try this for five to ten rounds, and then just sit quietly in meditation. You'll be surprised at how relaxed your mind and body will be. The simple act of breathing deeply is really powerful. After some weeks of practice, you may wish to increase the length of the out-breath, and also the amount of time you hold the breath. But remember there should never be any sense of strain.

I am the only one here taking yoga and meditation seriously. Sometimes I wish I could exchange a few words with others who love doing the daily practices. But never mind, I still have my peace and love surrounding every day. All it takes is a small space for a great journey. That's the beauty of the whole thing, that you don't need anybody or any tools to reach this precious feeling that follows you through the day. I always put into my prayers that I wish to be transformed daily into a better person. I have found out that this is exactly what is happening to me. God gave me yoga and meditation to grant my wish that I've been asking for, for a long time.

My faith in God and the Universe has grown so much more. And some big changes in the last six to twelve weeks have occurred in my dreams. For many years I would always have nightmares. I always remember my dreams, so I see clearly that the nightmares are gone. I don't remember when I dreamed the last time of something negative. All my dreams are either neutral or good.

Since I have signed the paperwork for my transfer to Germany, I've been missing home more than before and often it goes through my mind now. I wish I could be already in Germany in better surroundings and quietness.

May God be with you wherever you go. Love and light,
Hans

....

Dear Hans,

Your latest letters were moving to read, because despite all the disturbances surrounding you, you are finding the core for your life through your meditation. It is special to hear how your prayers are being answered, and your faith has grown. What treasure you have found, treasure that will be with you all your life. I don't expect I need to say this to you, but this treasure needs continual feeding and nurturing, so keep on going with your daily practice, and your prayers, wherever you are!

Peace be with you,
Caroline

....

Dear Caroline,

I'm happy that you see improvement in my letters as I definitely see myself getting better. The yoga asanas, the ways of breathing, and the deepness of my peaceful meditation have improved so much in the last two years. I know that I'm only at the beginning and knowing that there is so much more to reach gives me real joy. If two years can do so much good work, I'm ready for the future to take in all it gives to me. Yoga and meditation have opened more doors for me. Before, I used to see everything through one window, now I feel like I have more choices. I'm open-minded, tolerate more and don't get angry like I used to get. Even if I would be the only person on earth doing yoga and meditation practice I could never stop again. I don't need more proof, I can feel it daily. IT WORKS.

I read the New Testament some years ago and I remember questioning many things Jesus said. Now, after taking part in spiritual practices I can understand him so much more. Many things, like you said, ring a bell now! Of course he was a great human being. His love, teachings and caring, I now realise, are all true. Probably much more than is written down. To grow and deepen my practice is what I'm looking forward to.

123

I've been off medication since first week of July and it's like I've never been on them. Life is just the same if not better.

Been really discovering pranayama lately more and more. Of course, I still get angry about things but I can definitely see the changes in my personality. When I started with my yoga and meditation practice two years ago I had a real problem with the noise surrounding me, but now I take it with a smile. Even the Thai guy next to me who sometimes snores, two years ago I felt like punching him on the nose and cursed him all the time. But now when he starts and I'm meditating I laugh or smile!

Thank you in so many ways. Love,
   Hans

....

Charlotte, HMP Eastwood Park

The psychiatrist here feels that I am a case for therapy rather than punishment as a year ago I was diagnosed with a bipolar disorder. Will you still be able to write to me when I am in a hospital for criminals with mental disorders rather than in prison? I do hope so.

The yoga routine you recommended makes me feel great. It is just what I need. With an extra towel in my room to use as a mat I can do more yoga in my cell.

Our yoga class here in Eastwood Park is currently under threat due to funding issues. We have all written a letter to the governor saying that it would be a great shame to stop the class as yoga becomes a way of life. With its physical and meditative dimensions, it is a real and practical tool for spiritual enlightenment and awakening.

Do I find it hard being in prison? Well, my incarceration in mental hospitals in the past has given me previous experience of tolerating being confined. I know how to just get on with it. If I had had a support network like yours when I first presented to a hospital I would have made a better recovery.

Mental illnesses often manifest as spiritual experiences, which can be turbulent. Sadly, patients are often put in front of psychiatrists, who attribute a label of disease to what is a rocky but positive process. They then try to convince patients that their experiences are not real, and do not work through the issues with them. Sadly, this often makes things worse.

Being confined in a low-stimulation environment can be used as a good spiritual tool. I cannot escape from myself and get caught up in distractions so I'm meditating and reading more than on the outside. A saving grace has been the library service. I have also made great peace with silence and feel internally calmer. I've learned that I'm being taught a lesson in coping with loneliness. It's bearable and another good spiritual exercise to go within myself and get to know the unadulterated me.

Antonio, HMP Lewes

OCTOBER

For nearly nine months, I have been practising meditation. I still can't define it properly – exciting, torturing, empty, full, unbearable, unmissable. Perhaps it is for its mysterious simplicity that I can't help but do it every day. Has it changed my life? Well, it's hard to tell, because prison changes you, no matter what.

Other forms of active meditation have also helped me stay focused and strong. Yoga for a start, but recently even tai chi. My body benefits, and my mind is usually lighter after practising.

What attracts me to these things is that they point towards freedom. It's not about believing something or hoping for some kind of future happy resolution of my troubles. It's more about looking for real freedom through self-discovery.

I may not be experiencing hours of bliss when flowing in silence with the breath, nor always be happy and calm. But at least now I can just look at myself and shut up, observing what goes on in my mind. So far, finding out that as problems and worries arise, they also cease. Like with breathing, when the mind manages to let go, everything flows on alright on its own.

DECEMBER

It's incredible how amazingly powerful, in both good and bad ways, our mind is. Since my arrival in prison, I decided that I would not waste this strange challenge and the best I could come up with was exploring the mind whilst trying to keep fit. When I started meditating, I could barely sit for ten minutes. Now, I train my mind through meditation and yoga for longer periods, usually twice a day.

Throughout this sentence, my first, there have been difficulties. Many times I felt low, many times I felt I was not 'good enough' in my practice. Sometimes I would miss my family or I would feel sorry for causing a big hassle to them by coming to jail. But this practice has made me realise that suffering, craving, unsatisfactoriness, expectations and all possible states of mind or feelings arise, exist and pass away right here, inside my mind. They are not in the prison, they are the children of my own self, that I've built day after day.

Whatever I do and wherever I look, I see the constant action of my ego and my inner demons. I am not really happy, but I'm fairly calm and I want to face my mind full on. I feel a bit like Arjuna in the *Bhagavad Gita*: slightly sad and full of questions because I can't help but fight what has been my 'family' (conceits, ideas, beliefs, views, etc.) but I also feel the greatness of this opportunity. Up until my sentence I thought that being free meant freedom to do as you please. Up until last month I was thinking that knowledge was something intellect could master, but realise that true knowledge transcends thought and explanations.

Sometimes, I ask myself what will happen in two months, when I'll be released. How should I fit my practice with whatever life expects of me? On one side I'm tempted to simply allot the practice a bit of time, whilst trying to be mindful in my daily activities, but going back nonetheless to pursue worldly goals. On the other side, I fear to admit to myself, I may be actually tempted to make my practice the central part of my life. I guess wisdom regarding how to practise afterwards will only be available when those days come. In the meantime, let's not forget a valuable teaching of prison life: Take one day at a time.

One of the biggest insights I had recently could be phrased, 'You may not have an answer, but you can't not have the question.' So, even if exploring my mind and trying to liberate it may be scary at times, and forces me to face my most insidious fears, I feel I can't give up right now.

Be patient toward all that is unsolved in your heart and try to love the questions themselves...

Live the questions now. Perhaps you will gradually, without noticing it, live along some distant day into the answer.

Rainer Maria Rilke,
Letters to a Young Poet

JANUARY

At the moment, I usually do one hour of yoga and breathing exercises in the morning, followed by sitting meditation – between 20 and 50 minutes. Then I try to practise when I eat, brush my teeth, walk in the yard or work in the workshop. In the evening, if I have gym, I cool down with tai chi. Otherwise I just read. Just before bed I do some more sitting, about 20 minutes.

If there is one thing that I'm learning from meditation and yoga it's that the best way to prepare for the future is to live each moment grounded in the present. Speculating over what we can't be sure of is something my mind still ends up doing. So I guess that I will try and concentrate on making the best out of these last eight weeks in prison.

My father is coming to stay with me for a week when I'm released. He is a man with a great heart and his Christian faith has recently turned from a dogmatic set of beliefs to something more open-minded. I remember when he told me about his memories of his own father dying in his arms. He is very concerned with death. Neither hard work, nor taking care of the family's well-being, can – alone – help with his doubts and questions about the end of life. When I talked about meditation in our last conversation, he said, 'I wish I had five minutes to sit doing nothing, son.'

SUMMER 2015

I hoped I would write to you as a free man, but as you can see this is not the case. The Home Office decided to keep me in custody beyond the terms of my sentence, which is absurd because I've won my immigration case. What was worse is that a clerk from the Home Office came to see me one week ago and told me I was going to be released. This information had been given to the prison and to my probation officer too, so that everyone was surprised and disgusted when I received the letter that prevented my release. The Home Office sent it right on the evening before I would have left. By that time my dad had come all the way from Italy and my friends here had booked Tuesday off from work.

What my practice teaches me is that there is no benefit in planning too much for the future or believing too much in expectation. I should not have let my mind get too excited. But after my father and my friends visited me on Monday and my probation officer confirmed I was going to be released, I just couldn't help but let myself caress the idea of going back out there. And as I did so, life struck one of its lessons about non-attachment.

The prison's yoga teacher came to see me on that day, so he helped me detach from both frustration and physical feelings of anger. I couldn't sleep much, but I gathered myself together, got down to the floor and began to let tension find a way out in powerful asanas like warrior and crow. On Wednesday I managed to appreciate the importance of the insights I could get from my suffering. Today I managed to forgive both the Home Office and life in general.

What is happening remains totally unfair, but I don't have to identify with thoughts of bitterness. I chose to let go of thoughts of resentment and to let my inner sense of well-being emerge even in the midst of troubles. Mental discipline and understanding that the bigger picture is always more important than the passing details have been fundamental for finding peace and spiritual growth despite the external challenges. Now my practice has truly received the test of time. Through a mindful approach to uncertainty and hardship I am now freer and stronger than ever.

What you wrote me last time makes even more sense now; and when the day comes for me and my family to be reunited, I will simply share my life with them and let my silent example speak for itself.

Although I can't deny that experiencing bliss while meditating on my reaction to the 'bad' news of these days seemed very illogical and awkward at first, it definitely showed me some deep truth. You said that after release I 'simply' need to let my life become my practice, rather than trying to daydream now about what I should or should not do. No need to worry, right? At the end of the day all I have, really, is the present moment, so let's keep my practice rooted in the present.

I've stuck the letter from the Home Office up on the wall of my cell. I'm doing everything I can to fight for my release. I don't need to suffer for what I can't change. I don't need hatred.

I don't need anger. I don't need to keep making up stories about a self who doesn't deserve 'this' and will only be truly happy out of prison. I look at the paper and I don't feel anything, and somehow this lack of feeling feels good!

Connor

While I was in Waterstone's the other day, I bumped into a doctor who was my psychiatrist all the time I was locked up 12 years ago. He was really friendly, and asked me how I was getting on and what I was doing these days, and when I kept addressing him as doctor, he said, 'Please call me John.' He said it was good to see how his former patients were doing in life, especially when they were doing well, as I seemed to be. My new girlfriend was with me at the time as well, and he shook hands with her and wished her well. It was an uplifting experience.

I seem to be picking up in mood and progress quite quickly these days. It would be easy for me to get caught up in the gimmicky world of computers, hi-definition TVs and mobile phones, but I try to keep my feet firmly on the ground if I can.

No experience in my life matches the inner light and the calmness and peace which accompanies it, which I saw for a few hours when I had been close to death at the age of 26. That little pinpoint of light guides me through my life and has slowly, over a period of many years, brought me to the place in life where I am now, from a state of utter and complete hopelessness and danger and self-persecution. I will never abandon that now even to the point of death. Following the light is my 'raison d'être'.

At times I experience being at peace with things quite deeply; while at other times, things get in the way. It can be frustrating because when you experience peace, it's such a great feeling that you want it to stay with you all the time. Then seemingly for no reason it slips away and life's problems encroach on you and disturb things. It is quite important at those times to not get too frustrated with this.

There is no such thing as perfect peace lasting from our early days right up to the end of our lives. This frustrating loss of a peaceful feeling can get you down, so I see my challenge as making sure it doesn't defeat or discourage me.

Love

Once a friend wrote from prison, saying he was starting 'to think and feel for people with a clean feeling of love'. After a lifetime of using drugs, he had cracked, with everything going dark, only a flicker of light remaining. Since then, meditation had allowed him to clear his mind for the first time in many years, he said. It helped him discover this love for himself, and for other people, despite 'us never having had any love as kids'.

If you're among the huge number of people who feel hopeless some of the time, you might have caught yourself wondering: is it possible for me to know love, given how little of it I was shown growing up?

The letters in this section show that meditation and the right kind of support help you tap into a love both for yourself and other people. Some of the time, that love is very general, like Dave whose letters show how much he cares for the natural world, despite always feeling an outsider himself.

Other people find they start naturally expressing a kindness and openness to everyone, even potential enemies. One man told us he accidentally bumped into someone in the library one day, who threateningly growled, 'Watch it, arsehole!' He said because he himself kept his cool, there was no violence. Later that day, the growler approached him with genuine respect for how he'd conducted himself, wanting to know his secret. Love in this sense is a feeling of kindness towards everyone, even people who are threatening or annoying you, realising that they are just like you: with difficulties of their own, and often reacting out of habit or fear.

Still other people find themselves actively reaching out to other people, like one man who wrote from Haverigg prison saying that as a result of his practice, he was spending more time with newcomers, showing them the ropes and helping them feel less isolated.

Many of us find love a hard word to use; maybe it wouldn't be your first choice to describe these kinds of feelings. George, for example, uses the phrase 'joy of the heart'. In fact, it's not so important what word you use. It's far more important to just sit and find it for yourself, without words.

George, HMP Lowdham Grange

Hello there,

I have been doing yoga in Belmarsh. The teacher's name is Simon. I have come to respect Simon as every week I learn more and more. As I go deeper into yoga and meditation (which I find very hard) it seems to be bringing up all kinds of emotions. For example, last week after two hours with Simon, I came back to my cell and cried my eyes out. Is this normal?

I am reading the Bible as well and am really trying to find my spiritual side as well as get rid of this sadness that is deep inside me. I am working so hard on myself, but all these feelings scare me so much. I have been to the bottom, even tying a sheet round my neck six months ago. I know you have to go to the very bottom to get back up and believe me, I have been there.

I hope I have not wrote this all wrong. I have not done this before.
George

....

Dear George,

Thanks for telling us about yourself. You haven't got anything wrong in your letter. In fact, you have written a very moving and sensitive letter. It was completely appropriate and I was glad to be asked to reply.

What a journey you are taking. I'm not surprised you find it a rocky road, but you are so right in trying to go deeper with yoga and meditation as a way of coming to terms with your emotions and yourself. It takes courage, and although yoga and meditation bring up past hurts and sadness, gradually you will find that your courage increases. Your yoga teacher and we here at the Trust are here to help you on your journey.

The yoga classes are obviously uncovering all sorts of things for you, and it is quite normal to be in floods of tears as things come up. The journey you are taking will be a painful process, but I have a feeling you already realise how crucial it is for your well-being. It's like taking out a splinter. When the splinter is inside, it hurts. Once out, the pain goes. In the same way, while a hurt is inside you, it hurts. Take it out, look at it, give it an airing – and let it go (even if it means lots of tears). Your journey will probably bring up all sorts of things that you hadn't realised were there, or how deep they are, so it does require courage. And I know how hard it is to let go. It can take many, many times to look at the 'splinter' that is hurting – but letting go can only be good. Gradually, gradually, as you practise yoga and meditation you will find peace of mind.

Looking forward to hearing from you again. Go well,
  Caroline

....

Dear Caroline,

Thank you so much for your reply. When I started reading it, little tears flowed freely down my face. To say I wrote a moving and sensitive letter. For someone who does not know me to see that in me moved me very deeply. When these tears flow, I can't quite understand it. I think I am too old, I shouldn't be crying.

You see, mostly I was brought up, if you can call it that, in homes and care. But I have tried to make good. When I was at home I cried so much from the beatings and no love that I just gave up crying. I had no more tears left and now it's like, no George, keep it down, keep it down, must not be weak. To say I had a hard childhood is an understatement. I did not have one at all.

I have two beautiful boys I love very deeply and who have been brought up with so much love and safety. I feel ashamed of myself that I cannot be there for them. That is hurting me very much and them too, no doubt. Being locked up I can kind of handle. It's all that goes with it that's hard, if you know what I mean. I do not have self-pity.

The yoga we get on Monday and Thursday afternoons can be very hit and miss as to whether the prison has enough staff on to let it happen. So it is up to me in my cell. When I first went to yoga class I thought yes, just stretching and help keep fit. But now I read the Bible every day and try to meditate, which is the place that I really want to go but even understanding meditation is so very hard: Where is it going? What does it do? Will all the pain be worth it?

Is it about trying to keep your mind blank so that you can get the splinter out? Is it important to do the yoga first or can you just meditate?

I am very insecure. I know my girlfriend has been lying to me on the phone. I have only seen my boys twice in a whole year. I wrote this letter as well to try to lift my stress and it has worked a bit, so thank you. I shall now try to meditate and pray for peace inside and see how we go.

Peace and love,
George

....

Dear George,

What a wonderful letter. Although you say you are insecure, it takes a great deal of courage to write such a letter. You say you can't understand the tears, but hearing about your childhood, and the sadness of not seeing your two boys, brought tears to my eyes, and I am older than you! It is not unusual for this to happen when you are inside, being on your own (so to speak) and having the time to think about things. Do you think your tears are part of the letting-go process of past and present hurts? A sort of washing through? Tears can also be a sheer longing for love. Does it seem like that for you? If you see tears as a purification, that will transcend pity.

I can so appreciate that you find yoga and meditation difficult, but please take heart and keep going. You wonder about the value of doing yoga, and I would say the value of yoga is that the exercises bring well-being and harmony to the body, which in turn brings balance and harmony to the mind. To illustrate this, if you are not at peace in the mind, then you wobble when trying to balance on one leg! – so harmony in mind, harmony in body.

And you ask about meditation. The more you practise, the more the pain and tears will recede. It can be a long, slow process, but gradually, gradually, you will come to discover the benefits. It is best to practise meditation daily, focusing on the breath, and to practise yoga when you can. Do you focus on the breath at other times when you are not meditating? For instance, when you feel emotional or stressed? Are you noticing your breath as you read this?

You mention you have started reading the Bible and praying, and that also shows how much you are doing to turn your life around. Have you thought of talking to a chaplain? They are very experienced in listening to people and it may be something you would consider doing. It might be a great help to you to talk face-to-face with someone, in addition to writing letters.

Looking forward to hearing from you. Go well,
Caroline

....

Dear Caroline,

When I was in Belmarsh, my journey got very, very hard, with court and things. That is over and I am doing ten years now. I got my A Cat lifted (Yippee!) and two years has already passed. Where does it go? The sad thing is that in prison we wish our lives away.

After about 40 counselling sessions, I am starting to understand that I am a survivor, not a victim. All the help I've received, and everything I'm coming to understand about my past and myself, makes me want to go back out and do something good in my life for other people. But first I must finish fixing myself, which believe me is not easy.

I do know the path I want to be on. But some days the cloud is so dark it scares the life out of me and just carrying that around is such a great burden.

Looking forward to hearing from you. Kind regards,
George

....

Dear George,

It is very good to hear from you again. It sounds as if things are beginning to improve for you now. It must make a difference no longer being A Cat.

But it seems the real difference has been made through your courage and determination to come to terms with yourself and your own life, and then in turn to do something good for others. That is a truly inspiring thing to say. The path you have chosen has its ups and downs, but it sounds to me as if you have already taken many steps along that path with very positive results. I am sure it is not easy for you a lot of the time, and that some days are like being in dark clouds. What shines through your letter is courage!

Go well, go gently,
    Caroline

....

Dear Caroline,

One of the decisions I've made in recent months is to help others in need. If I can even just do a small amount of what I want to do, I know it will help many a person. This is in my heart so strongly, and I know one thing that I do have waves and waves of is empathy. That's because of all the suffering that I went through. Before I could offer my help, the one thing that I have had to do is fix myself, which, with lots of hard work, I am getting there.

When I got your newsletter I was in great shock to see my letter which I'd given you permission to print there. At first I didn't even want to come out of my cell because I was so worried what people would say, as counselling is a very personal thing to someone like myself. But now I am proud of it, to be chosen by you, and not ashamed.

My childhood nightmare was not my choice. If it had been, I would have rather been put down at birth. It seems to me that lots of public people do not understand the pain you have to go through to get over the pain. It is easy to see why people would rather cover it up with drink and drugs and other things. At the moment there is so much press about celebrities and important people being accused of crimes against children and young adults. Everyone waiting: who's next? Do they really care about us, the victims? What we have to carry around with us for so long? But through the help of yoga and meditation and lots of reflecting, it helps to let go, find enlightenment, and then move on, and lead a better life.

All my love,
George

....

Dear George,

I am so sorry you have been on a long and difficult journey. It is good that you have found yoga and meditation helpful. You make a valid point about the effect abuse has on victims, asking whether there is care for the victims. Possibly part of the trouble is that the press make much of the big names, and the care for the victims gets little attention, but there are many, many people who quietly go about trying to help victims. But as you know yourself, healing is a long, slow process.

I hope this brings encouragement for your own continued journey. Go well, go gently,
Caroline

....

Dear Caroline,

Meditation is such a battle. I am not always disciplined enough, and maybe not knowing and understanding about it totally. One of the hardest things on this journey is as you work so hard on yourself, and you think, 'Yes, at last I am going forward!' then bang! You get negative news and it sets you back so much and it's like, why can life be so unfair at times? What is the bloody point?

I find it hard to even look in the mirror. Maybe some advice on how to like yourself and to let people in more?

God bless you,
George

....

Dear George,

You are right when you say that meditation is a battle, and that the battle is with yourself, and that also meditation requires discipline. To realise both these things shows how mature you are with your meditating. However, the more you practise, the more you come to realise that the battle doesn't last, or rather the battle can come and go! It might help if you could change your thinking from it being a battle, to thinking of meditation as acceptance – of yourself as you are. This will make a surprising difference, not only to your practice, but to so much else in your life. Is this something you've realised already?
George, keep on going. You are doing so well.

Peace be with you,
Caroline

....

Dear Caroline,

One of the toughest battles that I have *is* acceptance of myself. Even just to look in the mirror is very hard. I don't look to see what is there. The first time as a child I leaned up on the bathroom sink at home to look in the mirror, the sink pulled away from the wall (it was old, or just poor workmanship). Well let me tell you, it was a long, long time before I looked in a mirror again. My dad got hold of me, hanged me upside down over the top bannister, bouncing me up and down, deciding whether to drop me or not. I was very scared. In the end, he just gave me a good hiding instead, which was not so bad I guess.
Wow. I've never written that before. I can remember it as if it was yesterday.

Last week I was sitting in my cell watching a DVD called *Playing for Keeps*. A big part of the story is about the love that the dad has for his son. So beautiful. As I was watching, the tears just started flowing out of me and my heart felt so strange, empty. You know, like when you get hunger pain in your stomach.

This really was a very, very heavy moment. It was like I knew for the first time what a broken heart really feels like. I never done anything with my father, like playing football, homework, reading a goodnight story. Nothing. Just nothing. But when we are born, we need love and plenty of it and to be *shown* love.

I understand and have so much empathy for people's pain and feelings, it goes so deep it even hurts me. It's one of the reasons that I believe I have so much to offer. How it will happen, I am not sure, but once that door opens it will be a great and amazing new chapter in my life, the best part of it, to bring all that shit into positive and do so much good for others.

God bless you,
George

....

Dear George,

I felt honoured you could write about your childhood in such an open way. I can so understand the traumas you felt as a child, and the longing to be loved by your father. The longing for love is so fundamental, isn't it?

It seems to me that you are so much on the right track of turning things around for yourself, even though there may seem to be so many difficulties, and your approach is spot on.

Your past will always be part of you, but it is a matter of accepting it, and letting go of it, which in turn becomes part of accepting yourself. This is where meditation comes in and why we recommend focusing on the breath, to bring you fully into the present moment. Is this something you find as you meditate?

Looking forward to hearing from you again. Go well,   141
Caroline

....

Dear Caroline,

I am so desperate to put my future into helping others, and I just really believe that I will as I have so much to offer and give, and what do I want in return? Just a little bit of true genuine happiness inside, and peace. What does that feel like Caroline? Do you have it? How does it feel?

The time ticks on till my freedom comes, but true freedom from myself and all the pain that I carry – will that ever come? It can be very hard getting up to face the day sometimes. What a bloody waste.

See, if I had had the right guidance in life and a bit of love, I really believe I would not be in this position. Not that I blame anyone else for my actions. But looking at it in another way, I am thinking that it was meant to be – all that suffering – as my real true journey of helping so many is going to start soon. All that negative into a true positive. Which will stop some future generations sitting in my position in years to come.

With kind love and respect,
   George

....

Dear George,

Your wish to reach out to others in order to help future generations to avoid the sort of experiences you had is excellent. You talk about reaching a little bit of 'true genuine happiness inside, and peace'. Can I gently remind you that what you need – genuine happiness and peace – is with you all the time? And it is with everyone and is intrinsic. It is not fleeting, but is instead a sense that all is okay, despite the difficulties of being alive. Once this is discovered, peace can be found in the most challenging places, even in prison.

How to reach this state of peace and genuine happiness? One of the best and proven ways is through meditation. Have you glimpsed (or had a deep sense of) this when you have meditated? I think you probably have, but I would love to hear from you yourself.

When you say you wish to help others, have you realised this can happen right now? For some reason you have been placed amongst people who really need help, guidance, acceptance and love. Perhaps you can see this opportunity with you right now, and understand the potential you have to make life easier to everyone around you.

Can I suggest another way of building up positive thought and confidence? At the end of each day, think of three things that have happened during the day to say thank you for. It could be something as simple as being given a smile by someone. But however bad the day might seem to have been, still find three things to say or write thank you for.

Peace be with you,
Caroline

....

Dear Caroline,

I am now in Cardiff. Talk about being tested. A Cat to D Cat, now back to B Cat. But I am staying strong and making good out of a bad situation.

Since I've been in Cardiff, my help to others has increased greatly. Being part of the Listening Team and a peer advisor, I get a good feeling from helping others, and no matter what, I have come on in myself so much.

I still spend a lot of time looking into myself, understanding myself and weakness and my bad side, then working on improving myself as I know there are challenging times ahead and the future is a worry for me. I do have a plan. But just to lead a law-abiding life is going to be a challenge, being I've spent all my life being a crook and trying to perfect it. The big negative is, I will be 50 years old. I worry about time running out to be able to prove myself.

Last week was four years to the day of the death of my dad. So I spoke to my mum for the first time in many years. She was very shocked. I rang to let her know that I forgive her. It really was a very powerful moment, and something I never thought I was capable of doing. She herself is very ill with cancer and I'm not sure if I will see her again. But what I would say is that the power of forgiveness is a difficult journey to get through, but the reward at the end for all parties is something else. Forgiveness is something people should do more of, just for themselves, as it really does help you move on and shows how far you have come.

All the best,
   George

....

Dear George,

Don't worry about becoming 50, and running out of time to prove yourself! There is tension, to become the person you think you should be, and needing time to do it. However, there is always time, and that is why it is so important to live 'in the moment' and be totally aware of the moment, living it to the full. This is where change happens. This is where stability lies. This is where peace lies. But I think you know this already, from reading between the lines of your letter.

It does take courage to live in the moment! Well, you have shown courage by getting in touch with your mum, and showing you forgive her. What a powerful moment it must have been. It shows how far you have come.

Go well, go gently,
   Caroline

....

Dear Caroline,

I have learnt it is better to have joy in your heart than happiness. All this time I was searching for happiness, but that just comes and goes. It is joy of the heart that will fill you up and stay with you no matter how tough things get in life.

I came to recognise this joy in a sort of light-bulb moment. I was in church and some guy was talking about joy this, joy that, and I thought, 'Oh my God, I got it all wrong.' See, I had been searching for happiness, when I used to get counselling I was searching for happiness. But I got an emptiness deep inside and I've tried but it won't let me go. This is an emptiness that I have always had, starved of love, kindness, and happiness. So I realised that it's like looking for Genghis Khan's burial plot. I am never going to find it, because I was looking at it all wrong. I have been happy lots of times. It comes and goes. New suit, come into money? Yes, happy.

But joy. Well, that is so different. When my sons were born, that's joy. It is the joy that I have been blessed with that was always there – just never understood – that has kept me going through, as you say, all the ups and downs. Joy of the heart. What a very beautiful thing to have. We all have it. We just have to open our hearts.

My release date coming soon is getting me very worried and even to the point of being scared. The day I got arrested five years ago, so much was going on in my life and I have lost most of it. I will be 50. I know it will never be the same.

I will rise like a Phoenix and my time to shine is coming. I have so much to give. Greatest respect to you. Thank you, thank you, thank you,

George

....

Dear George,

By the time you read this you will be out of prison. I am not surprised you were feeling anxious about your release. Perhaps now you are out, perspectives are changing, but from what you say in your letters, there are challenging times ahead.

You have explained so well the difference between happiness, that is often fleeting and illusory, and genuine joy, that just is. We can all be swept into looking for happiness, can't we? Keep working on 'joy of the heart'.

The challenge for you is to sustain the changes you've made, now that you are out. One that you seem to have really worked on is forgiveness. It is a crucial element, isn't it, for all relationships, a complex issue, one that is ongoing. I hope you find the strength and courage to continue your path of forgiveness and letting go.

Perhaps becoming 50 will be a good thing! Perhaps you will see things from a different perspective and discover new priorities. Although I can see that your release is looming large. It will be a big change, and I can understand you feeling scared.

Try and keep to a regular daily practice. I know this is harder when you are no longer in the routine of prison, so it becomes even more important to build up your own regular time. Meditation is hard, isn't it? But it is a healing practice.

With all best wishes,
   Caroline

....

Jack, HMP Wakefield

Dear Ava,

Thanks for your latest letter. My weight problem needed actioning, so I managed to get myself on prescription gym and weight management classes. With my extra energy from not smoking I can give the gym all I've got and am pleased to report the weight is dropping off. I'm watching what I eat and really enjoying relaxing with my meditation books.

If I can crack the weight issue along with the smoking (already done) I'll have come so far. I am even running again, doing laps around our sports field. This is all down to confidence in what I have found in myself through your books. I really do feel so confident, which is refreshing as I would normally give up when it comes to diet and exercise. I really am beginning to feel free.

Prison is so much of a roller coaster, one minute up, the next down. I'm currently very much on the up. My times of meditation have become much more relaxed than they ever were. The future's looking a lot rosier.

However, my family have disowned me and that hurts. I have to respect their wishes, though. I sometimes feel so low about that but I have to keep going.

Christmas is coming and, despite being in prison, I always enjoy it. Me and a friend club together for a buffet which we prepare and invite people to come and enjoy with us. We buy little toiletry items from the canteen and wrap them up to open on Christmas day. We may not be out yet but we will do our best with what we've got. It brings tears to my eyes when I receive gifts from people at Christmas, just to say thanks for me being there for them all year.

With thanks for your friendship,
    Jack

....

Dear Jack,

It's marvellous that you've managed to give up smoking. It's hard enough 'outside' with lots of support. If you do slip back, don't give yourself a hard time, will you? Do you ever get a chance to go outside and look at the sky and the clouds and listen to the birds and take some deep breaths?

It sounds really hard, your family giving up on you. It is completely natural that you would feel low about this. Do you think it is possible to stay open and loving to them in your heart, even though you may not be in touch? While you can always hope that one day you might establish relationships with them, clinging too fiercely to this will just bring you pain. But do bear in mind that even the biggest family rifts are sometimes healed over time. The kind of internal work you are doing on yourself often helps to make this possible.

Your relationship with your family will continue even if you aren't in contact, as they have been a big part of your life, and you will continue to think of them and be affected by them, and they by you. Keep building on your practice and become as robust as you can be in preparation for what lies ahead.

You will be able to take all your experiences and understanding of others with you when you leave. What a wonderful thought!

Sending you warm good wishes, Jack,
    Ava

....

Dave, HMP Featherstone

Dear John,

I'm still trying to get my head around this seven-and-a-half-year sentence. It's getting a bit easier to accept. My mum now 82 is finding this one hard and thinks she has lost me for ever.

I always make plans that are destined to fail and when they do, I punish myself and feel worthless. If I do something good – a painting, a poem, a good turn, save someone's life – I hide it or deny I have anything to do with it. But if it goes wrong, everyone has to know.

What's wrong with me? I can't take praise or reward, keep feeling shit, worthless, and excel under stress and negative criticism yet I always hid my true thoughts, feelings and emotions. I also isolate myself as often as I can. The outsider, the odd one out. Why do so many people hate me and want to inflict violence on me just because I am different? Why can't I find peace outside myself in society?

Sharing an 8 by 12 foot cell with an inconsiderate man with a hygiene problem who lives for gangster rap, soap operas, sex and drugs is extremely frustrating and it's all too much thinking it's going to be like this for the next three to five years. God. Give me peace. I'm 50 and can't handle much more of this.

I had a father who ignored me and mentally abused me, always putting me down, a bully and coward. Yet Mum was kind, loving and wonderful. I was violently sexually abused by another man at nine. And school was hell, always being tormented to the point of attempting suicide. A dead end job at 15. A loner with no mates. A wife who turned into a woman possessed and was unfaithful. So, divorce. Nine years in the British Army witnessing and having to take part in extreme violence in Africa, Beirut, Northern Ireland and Central America. Being kidnapped and tortured for three days. Witnessing the life-crippling injuries of my only son. The body of my only brother all cut up, violently murdered. Living rough the past 12 years and seeing eight of my friends killed or die on the streets. Fighting and beating my alcohol addiction. And in and out of prison.

I'm so in touch with the beautiful earth and I have done so much for animal care, tree planting, bird and butterfly conservation, waste limitation, recycling and I put my love into it all. Now I'm 50 and with a heart condition I don't think I'll last much longer. So, why has it been like it has? And how can I use the rest of my life?

Love ya,
Dave

....

Dear Dave,

It must be very hard for your mum, but she still has you to write to. She obviously loves you to bits and you will no doubt send her equally comforting letters. If she can keep you in her thoughts and you do the same, it is as though you are one, which you are. Your letter which started with the devastating news that you have to do seven-and-a-half years warmed my heart by hearing of your love for the earth, its trees and animals. This reflects your sensitivity and spirituality. Love and acceptance can be felt easily by us in nature, but we generally feel it from fellow humans when we stop worrying about it. Then it often comes when least expected. I think many sensitive people consider themselves to be outsiders, but we are all part of a whole, and the more we explore our spirituality, the clearer that becomes.

In your earlier letters, I see you reaching for good when life has dealt you such a hard hand. You look for peace even in an 8 by

12 foot cell with a difficult roommate. Your consideration for the environment is inspiring. Do you think you can develop this in prison? I would like to hear what you are thinking we can do to help this poor old earth, I really would.

Do try some of the breathing exercises and meditation and let me know how you get on. Meanwhile, I will be sitting with you in spirit, as I am sure your good mother is doing.

Love,
   John
....

John,

Yes the breathing exercises work for me when I am able to practise them. Like the few minutes seated before I turn on my machine in computer literacy and IT skills class, or when the light is out and I am in bed.

Just a few things we can all try to do to help this earth: recycle, recycle, recycle. Give back to the earth what you have to take away. Say thanks to Mother Nature. Never kill, even insects; they, like us, are all clinging to life, day by day. Only eat what you need. Don't waste food or water. Walk slowly, stay calm.

Peace and love to all,
   Dave
....

Exercise: Lengthening the Out-breath

Here's a powerful breathing exercise, similar to the one Dave used. Try it now, and know that it really helps when you feel anxious or depressed. Remember not to try too hard, but just enjoy the relief of slowing down and being truly present as you do it.

1. Sit in one of the positions described in the first part of this book. When you breathe in, let it come in slowly as you count to five. Now breathe out slowly, again counting to five.

2. At the end of every out-breath, wait. Because we breathe in automatically, we never need to worry about the in-breath. It will arrive on its own. This wait, this pause before the next in-breath, is like the still centre of a turning wheel. It is precious. Enjoy it. It may last anything from a second to five seconds. Let it occur naturally.

3. And now repeat, breathing in as you count to five, and breathing out as you count to five. Do this for five rounds.

4. On the sixth round, breathe in as you count to five, but now breathe out more slowly as you count to ten. You will have to use some control to make the out-breath twice as long, but you can do it.

5. Keep going like this for ten rounds or even up to 30 minutes if you wish: breathing in for five, breathing out for ten.

Afterwards, let go of counting and controlling the breath, and just appreciate simple, natural breathing. It's great to carry on after this, moving seamlessly into silent meditation, staying with each in-breath, each out-breath. Even though life around you may be full of noise, you'll find stillness and peace.

Dear Dave,

In your earlier letters you mentioned feeling worthless. The best way I have found to build self-esteem is to meditate. I cannot really explain why, but when you sit in meditation, you are not trying to achieve anything. You're not trying to be better or good. You are giving yourself some real quality time, pausing to tune into the universe as a whole and listen to the quiet. Perhaps you will try it and let me know what you hear. Because although there are doors slamming, people shouting, sound systems blasting, there is still that quiet to be found within yourself.

Just focusing on the breath leaves little or no room for all the other noises and distractions and that lets all that stuff, which makes us think we need to be better, just drop away; the real stuff gets a chance to manifest itself and to show that the real Dave is just PERFECT! Try it for yourself and discover this. I will be sitting with you. It's nice to know that when anyone of us sits, we never sit alone.

Love from us all,
  John

....

John,

Hi. Thanks for your encouraging letter. I am angry and can't seem to turn it around. All the therapeutic work and education is only on offer to those doing two years or under. So I have to now sit putting four tea bags, four sugars, four milks in a plastic bag all f*****g day for £5 a week. And I still have to share a cell with someone who has no consideration for others at all.

I can't find out anything here about a yoga class or meditation time. I can't get hold of any art and craft materials to use in my cell and library never gets called. I'm banged up with a football and Big Brother addict who fills the cell with as many useless possessions as he can. They promised me it would get better.

One of Dave's recycled envelopes

I feel crushed and trapped physically, mentally and emotionally. I'm trapped in a world of fierce neglect with a great desire to help but I cannot. HELP! What's happening? Where am I going? What do I do?

Dave

....

Dear Dave,

What a terrible time you are having. Is there anything you can say to your cellmate to negotiate a better deal for yourself, do you think? Could he have five hours for his stuff and you have five hours of what you prefer? You have such a good way with words and a deep understanding of nature: can you find out what makes him tick and plough a way through, which would keep the peace and improve things?

It is often said that inner peace is found in the strangest places; even in the stuffing of four tea bags, four sugars and four milks. May I suggest you use it as an exercise? Is it possible to let your mind just rest whilst you're working, just be aware of your breath, breathing in, breathing out, tuning all the other stuff out?

Love from us all to you and your mother. Hang in there Dave,
John

....

Dear John,

I was in a bad patch there for a while, but a day or two later I took a few steps back: who am I to complain? There is nothing that I need. Someone has to have them tea bags. If people don't want to listen to my requests, I can accept that. The breathing concentration is slowly working better now. I take any opportunity I can to practise it. I am definitely getting the clean feeling in my mind after, and the peace with the concentration is great.

Someone somewhere must have recognised my potential because last week I was given a Trusted Job as a Mentor teaching English to those who need help. It's so rewarding. I have four students: African, English (Romany), Vietnamese and an Asian guy, all doing well.

Today I went to the Buddhist service for the first time here. The simplicity of it and the peacefulness was so emotional I shed tears of joy and happiness. After meditation we had an extended chat and the teacher gave me a lesson to practise with the breathing and yoga techniques you gave me.

Hoping you find inspiration in all you do. Write soon,
Dave

....

Dear Dave,

It is really nice to hear that you are receiving a few good things at present like a greater sense of peace and concentration. Also that you are being given opportunities to help others and finding that fulfilling and worthwhile. Who was it who said, 'If you want to be happy, help the fellow next to you'?

Love from us all to you, and from me personally,
John

....

Hey John,

I have been coming off the anti-depressants I've been on for ages to help with post-traumatic stress disorder from my time in the army in Beirut and Lebanon. The meditation, breathing and self-control, used with the yoga, has guided me through. I am now experiencing real thoughts, feelings and emotions, and working through them in a positive way. I feel free now, with little weight to carry. Yes, I know it won't be like this always, but I feel more prepared. I must stay on this path somehow.

Now I've got my own pad and I've painted it. I've kept it simple, with the minimum of possessions and very lean. I meditate three times a day, and keep to a vegetarian diet.

I send peace and love you and all the team. In fact, I think I'll send it to everyone. Everywhere.

Dave

....

Dear Dave,

Your cell sounds like a monk's cell – plain and clean. What a great place to meditate. I admire you coming off the anti-depressants. It must be very difficult, like throwing away a crutch and standing on a mended leg without it. You are starting to feel again – not easy. I'm so glad the Buddhist services are there to support you.

Life is constant change, but there is no need to live future troubles. You know the expression, 'Don't cross your bridges before you come to them.' In the meantime, be and enjoy the present. Simple counting of the breath does not allow for future problems.

Sometimes when meditating we are told to sit mountain still. This summer I walked across a mountain and sat on the top for a while, just being quiet. Where I or the mountain began or ended I cannot say. Tell me in your next letter about what you need to get for your D Cat. I would be very interested to hear.

156 Congratulations, and love,

John

....

Hi John,

To be eligible for a Cat D prison, first you need commitment to change your life for the better. You must be willing to do anything probation tell you to, even if it goes against the work and plans you have made (which is the big crunch). It also helps enormously if you do a lot of bowing and scraping and arse kissing.

I'm struggling coming off the anti-depressants. One day I'm up, the next really down. Sometimes angry, other times emotional, other times feeling worthless, often confused. But trying to think positive, along with meditation, works for me. The TV has a lot of negative influence, so it stays off mostly.

My job as mentor gives me a huge feeling of self-worth which I have never had, even when I was in the army. I thought everyone else was fitter, stronger, better, so I would do stupid dangerous things to prove myself. CRAZY, huh?

Something must be changing in me, John, because I can't ever remember writing like this to anyone. I feel free to write whatever I like and listen closely to people's opinions.

Love to all,
Dave

....

Dear Dave,

The things you have to do to move to Cat D seem challenging. I've been reading some books by Alexander Kent about a boy in the 18th-century navy moving through the ranks. He has to kow-tow to the officers and the captain, however irrational they seemed. You would know about this much better than I, having gone through the army. Perhaps you are able to put your experiences there to work? Always remember the breath if someone annoys you: it really helps to take a few moments and to be aware of breathing, especially letting go on the out-breath.

As you say, something is indeed changing in you – just be patient with yourself.

Love,
John

....

Dear John,

It's been a week of very mixed emotions. I'm still angry at probation as they still continue to ignore all my pleas and applications. Not a single acknowledgement in 12 months.

Now, my teeth and jaw. Well, I could blame it on alcohol, drugs and the horrors of war but no-one made me do all that s**t. Alcohol numbed the emotional pain and the opiates killed the physical pain and ten years living on the street and in forests killed the pain of disassociation. Anyway, all my teeth are now worn down to the nerves but cannot be pulled out and it is affecting my jaw as I cannot chew or bite. I am now suffering stomach problems because all I can eat is soft or liquid food and bread. They have offered me codeine but I ain't never going to start that again. NO WAY MAN! The pain is constant and driving me slowly insane but I have suffered a lot worse, believe me. It makes me ill, angry and resentful, but all that goes away when I meditate.

I realise how privileged I am to be alive because there are so many beautiful times I have yet to experience. And I've got arms. Legs. I can see. Hear. Smell. Think. And I have peace of mind. I have food, clothes, shelter and – what I have come to know you as – a good, trusted friend.

Love and peace,
Dave

....

Max, HMP Glenochil

Max and Wendy have been corresponding since 2005. Their mutual concern and respect has become deep over time. While all of Max's letters are full of insight, this set of letters shows a particular challenge that some people experience when they set high standards for themselves.

Dear Wendy,

I'm a bit all over the place at this time. I have stopped meditating, only for the second time in five years. I'm questioning my ability to continue on this path. Truth is, I'm pretty shit at being a Buddhist. Many people come to speak to me every day. It's all about others, the system, how hard done they have been, on and on. This is taking its toll on me: as I try to listen, I feel myself being pulled in. I feel as though I'm sinking into the abyss.

Imagine you are in a large room with 100 other people and each is voicing their grievance with the world. You are trying to still the mind, yet at the same time appear interested in your fellow men. There are only three outcomes: (1) you manage to still the mind while sitting on a hornets' nest; (2) you give all your time to others, not through choice; or (3) you become part of the collective. I'm so sad to tell you that I feel as though I'm becoming pulled to number three. I can't seem to stop it. The Buddha said that if you put a piece of rosewood next to a piece of sandalwood, after a while they will start to smell like each other.

Do you understand what I am trying to say? I am at the bottom of the mountain again and I have no-one to talk to about it.

I am not lonely, though I feel alone. I am not depressed and yet I'm forlorn. There is a lot of confusion here. I understand nothing about life. Those 20 years that I spent as a hedonist were a simple, uncomplicated existence compared to this. I have been thinking of giving up my Buddhist study and joining the living dead again, yet something keeps me connected. I'm not sure what's going on any more. I'm waking up in the morning and I'm pissed off that I woke up again. I'm not that fussed about life any more. I'm not afraid of dying, and would not take my own life but would welcome death with open arms.

I have gone on long enough. I don't want you to worry. I will be fine, always am. I hope this letter finds you well and in good spirits. Take care,

Always your friend,
   Max

....

Dear Max,

My main concern is that you say you have stopped meditating. I can well imagine that by the time you get this, you have taken it on again as it seems that once you have begun to follow this way, it is actually quite hard to turn aside and feel at all comfortable or at ease walking down another.

It is a good moment for me to write these words as, having hurt my back, I have spent almost three weeks making an almost wholly unsuccessful effort to meditate lying on the floor. It should be possible, but what stopped me was being so focused on myself and my back predicament. I found it almost impossible to enter that space where the self is no longer in the forefront. I have felt increasingly grumpy and desolate as a result. But this morning I did sit on my cushion for half an hour. It is pathetic to think you can only meditate in one position – I am sure it is possible even doing bends, as you once described – but this afternoon I shall try just sitting cross-legged on my sofa.

People all around you who do nothing but grumble about the system sounds soul-destroying. First, I wonder what has put into your head the idea that you aren't much good at being a Buddhist. All these years, you have taught me so much about the essence of being a Buddhist that I can't quite imagine what you mean. All the people who want to unburden their hearts to you see something in you that you yourself seem to have lost sight of. Maybe you are just inventing an excuse about being useless because you have found yourself in a period of the 'dark night of the soul'. But you have always got through these times before and come out the other side all the stronger and more able to inspire others.

I can all too well imagine being in a large room with 100 other people all grousing away while you long to still your mind which, as you say, to do on a hornets' nest is rather a hefty challenge. And I also abhor the idea of just 'giving yourself to others' rather against your will and in a way that can make you feel superior. Your way of joining in is *much* the most generous actually, but Max, isn't the only way to do this to good effect precisely by gathering strength and wisdom by meditating each morning – even for ten minutes? Where can you get the inner strength you need, both to put up with everyone without feeling alienated from them and also to be able to give advice or encouragement that has some depth and insights, if it is not from your own inner depth, from being in touch with your very being and the very being of the universe?

That feeling of being at the bottom of the mountain must be one that everyone continues to feel from time to time all through life. But there is, we know, no bottom and no top to the mountain. We are where we are, there and nowhere, who we are – ourselves and no-one. All that matters is the silence, the depth – I know you don't think in terms of God, but Isaiah writes somewhere, 'Wait for God and God will give you strength and you will rise up on wings like eagles, you will run and not be weary, walk and not faint.' This is my heartfelt prayer for you.

I understand that feeling of 'not lonely and yet alone'. Being surrounded by people, or even being in a partnership with one, is no antidote to feeling alone. 'Forlorn' is such a good word to use to describe your present state. Forlorn, forsaken, abandoned, without hope. Wait, and hope will return 'as sure as the rain in spring or the dawn after the night'. As sure as that Max.

I also very well know the feeling of looking back and thinking that days with no feeling of pressure to spend time on meditation or one's inner life were simpler, freer, less complicated and confused. But it is, of course, all a complete delusion. Freedom? Simplicity? Tranquillity? A sense of purpose? Satisfaction? Contentment? There was none of that if we look even just below the surface, none of it. And my friend, you are the one who refers to that state as a 'living death'. I have suddenly thought that so much of what I have just written I have learnt from you in any case.

I totally trust you will be fine. But nevertheless I am sad if you wake up listless and not happy that the day has come. And I'm sad that you are going through a time of such turmoil.

This comes with all my warmest wishes possible,
   Wendy

....

Hello Wendy,

Things here aren't as good as they could be. I got to move to a cell away from the desk because it was noisy and also because the guy next to me played loud dance music, so all seemed fine at first but some young offenders are on the flat below. Now what has developed is cell wars. I don't want to bore you with the details but let's just say I had to resort to some childish behaviour in order to get them to see sense. Prison life can be so trying at times. That peace that I have always searched for just does not exist. I have stopped trying to look for rainbows. For six years I have put myself through such torment, only to fall once more. The spiritual life seems that bit too complicated while still in here. I have decided simply to meditate when I can. I will try to be a lot easier on myself. The thing is that I have been stressing myself out far too much over the last six years and I'm not prepared to do it any longer. I will put myself on the funeral pyre at this rate. I'm saying no. I have been trying to use this place as some sort of a monastery with me as a prison monk. It is not really possible, though it is possible still to do some good work with the mind.

One good thing is that I have been listening to music again. This might sound strange but I am going to start enjoying life again. I do really believe that I was making myself sad through the practice, and that can't be right. I have many tools for the mind that I have gained over the years and yet I don't use them. It would be fair to say that I have pushed myself too hard, which has caused me a lot of suffering in the past, as well you know.

This thing about letting go of the past: how difficult is that, especially when the past has been rather volatile?!? I suppose it's the same if your past has been colourful for better reasons. That's why you get people like the Rolling Stones still trying to rock it even though they are all touching their 80s. It is just as hard to let go of the good stuff as it is of the bad. Will we ever be set free?

It has taken me a long time to forgive myself for past actions but I do now forgive myself, for I know that the person who writes this is not the same person who did all that other stuff, though you are made to feel that way. But I'm the master of my fate, I'm the captain of my soul. In a Theravada[1] book I have been reading it says that all that is happening in your life is meant to be happening. So I am meant to be here. We are meant to find the spiritual life and then follow it, but it is no easy undertaking. Even if you find it, it is no honey to taste.

Love,
   Max

....

My dear friend Max,

I wonder if you have found a way of following your spiritual path that you feel is more compatible with life in prison. You sound as

---

1   A branch of Buddhism with long-established roots in Sri Lanka, Thailand, Cambodia, Laos and Burma.

though you have come to realise that you have been very strict with yourself over the last six years and that you can't go on at that level. Of course a prison isn't a monastery, but all the same, it is quite amazing how you have deepened your understanding and practice since you started it (was it six years ago?) and I am sure you will soon find a way, as you say, of carrying on doing 'good work to still the mind'. I am sure you will find a way because I am sure that, even if you have moments of resenting the discipline it needs and feeling that the noise and the culture and all the rest in prison are simply militating too hard against such an effort, you will never give up because you know that this is what has sustained you up to now and prevented you from sinking into childish behaviour – or worse – in the way that you see others doing around you.

It's lovely that you have started listening to music again. I think that the capacity (and will) to enjoy life is fundamentally important for any human being and if you are able to do that in prison, then all the better! It definitely can't be right to make yourself sad through the practice. Of course the peace and contentment it brings is on a different level from enjoyment of everyday things but the two aren't disconnected from each other.

When I have entered deeply into the emptiness within me is when I am most receptive to things like beauty and friendship and also enjoyment of things like music. Maybe you have something in your character that pushes you to extremes – a kind of 'all or nothing' trait. On the other hand, serious meditation practice cannot be something you dip into now and then when the mood takes you. There is no denying that it requires a completely regular discipline; but nor is it through our own will-power that the way to enlightenment, or even glimpses of it, is opened, but through the casting aside of our will and the letting go of any urge to achieve anything at all.

So maybe you have reached the point where you see you have been trying too hard and it is a question of just stilling your mind and being open to receive what is given to you rather than doing any active searching. All this is, of course, a lot easier said than done. It is so contrary to our Western culture where we think we have to manage everything, take charge, control our own destinies, etc. And the kinds of challenges you are up against in prison are unimaginable to me. I do think you are genuinely wonderful at dealing with them – not least with the boom boom of music all around you.

Take good care of yourself dear Max,
    Wendy

....

Dear Wendy,

I feel that God is far away from me at this time. I have hit a bit of a bad patch. My mind is not good. The tide of my mind has gone out but I do hope to welcome its return soon. It's not so much the prison, though that in itself is bad, but rather the people I have to live with. I'm having problems with another noisy neighbour and because I have tinnitus it can make it all the worse.

In that Kipling poem it says if you can keep your head when all about you they are losing theirs. That is no easy undertaking in this place. How on earth am I supposed to love my fellow man when I loathe him so terribly?

Is it the measure of the man I am by how I look upon others? Is it possible to understand someone who is difficult and thereby love him even if you still really loathe his ways? I keep thinking that God might be testing me and that if he is, I have failed again and again and again.

I really believe that it is all simply my karma catching up with me. That and also that it is by my negative thoughts I am bringing this to me. I really do not know how to be positive for long periods in this place. There are moments when I do feel good about my life but they are soon replaced by my surroundings and the reality of my situation.

I was woken up last night by people playing their radios, once at 12.30 a.m. and then again at 2 a.m. I tried not to let it bother me but it did, very much so. But then I thought of all the people in my life I have bothered with loud music and unnecessary noise and

I am so sorry to say it has been many. Before I came to prison, a woman came to my door one morning asking me nicely if I could keep the noise down at night as she had to work in the morning. I was so rude to her and shut the door in her face.

There are many examples of my selfish behaviour back then, but I was very much a different kind of person. I have moved on a lot and would like to think I am kinder in my manner but I do still have a heavy heart at times. I feel lost and trapped in a place like this. I am a recovering failure of a human being and I am not getting any help from the people who are supposed to be helping me.

Much love, your friend,
   Max

....

Dear friend Max,

It may seem to you that I am living in a sort of heartless cloud cuckoo land, insisting on meditation as the way forward when you have people near you making your tinnitus unbearable. But experience does tell me that inner peace is only to be found in inner silence and letting go of all anxieties and fears, in the knowledge that, whatever our frantic brains might be telling us, we are actually not in control of anything. Experience undoubtedly tells you that too, as I often think you have been able to enter into that inner silence very profoundly.

You say, 'The tide of my mind has gone out' and that you feel that God is far away. No doubt it seems a very dark, pitch-black night but, as some of the greatest mystics have said again and again, it is only after the night has been dark that the dawn can break.

God cannot be far away. It is impossible because the very nature and essence of God is all around you, in the air, the dust, the people (yes, even the noisy ones!) and above all within your very deepest self. That you can't perceive this at the moment doesn't change the reality. Those times when we are unable even to glimpse that reality are bleak, very bleak indeed. I know them well. But I am completely sure that, sooner or later, you will be 'welcoming the return of your mind again' (as you beautifully put it), and that your experience will be all the stronger, and more full of insights and hopefulness than before.

What about Psalm 139? 'Where can I go from your Spirit? Where can I flee from your presence? If I go up to the heavens, you are there; if I make my bed in the depths, you are there. If I rise on the wings of the dawn, if I settle on the far side of the sea, even there your hand will guide me, your right hand will hold me fast.'

It is not a question of your having failed, Max. What does 'failure' mean? We just live on as best we can, going astray, losing our way, getting tangled up in thistles and stinging nettles and then coming out again for a while into the sunlight and soft grass.

That you find it difficult to be positive for long periods in prison is not surprising. Lots of us here outside often find ourselves falling into negativity even though we are free and have trees and flowers and birds around us. It isn't all to do with the place, but it obviously makes it more difficult to be glad in life if you are locked up, especially with people who annoy you.

With love from your friend,
    Wendy

....

Hullo Wendy,

It brings warmth to my heart to be able to spend these lovely moments of my life with someone who I can be completely open with. When you have hidden so long from the world as I have done, it is difficult to allow yourself back in the game. Whether you are aware of it or not, you have played a big part in all of this. As have others. But for some reason you walked closest to me in all of this.

I have continued to experience some unusual things. Last night, for instance, I experienced during meditation the need for nothing at all. All wants, all desires, subsided. It was a feeling of liberation and fear also, rather an alarming success.

I have seen both sides of darkness and therefore it is easy, very easy, for me to gauge what's what. What I mean by this is that I have tasted something very real during meditation. Whatever it is, it far outshines anything that I have experienced in the past. LSD, ecstasy, dope, glue, booze, speed, cocaine, sex, partying. I think that by doing all these things I was trying to find something in my life; but by using those things, the light was much too bright, so it would bring me full circle back to the darkness, sometimes to places of tremendous darkness. In order to cope with these monsters inside I always needed to take more. And it took a man's life for me to finally get off this roller coaster of self-destruction. What a crazy web.

It would be nice to be able to sit down with someone and have a dharma[2] chat. To go over all the ins and outs of the process of the practice. I know that talk isn't where it's at when it comes to practice, but it does help whenever I get the chance. Although the Buddha's wisdom far outshines my own, I can understand how massive the task must have been to communicate to others what it meant to free oneself from oneself.

Each day I seem to be learning more, and the more I learn, the more I get hoodwinked and pulled hither and thither. Why does this mind keep jumping to this self of the past, of future, of day dream, of fantasy, of I said, he said, she said, should have said, etc.

Yes, yes! I do hear the birds each day. Every morning when I wake, the blackbirds are doing their morning song. When my mind will not settle during meditating I sit and listen to the feathered friends. On occasion I see a few swans go by. When I look out of the window I see them with the Ochil Hills behind them, truly a wonderful sight to see. I hear the crows and the starlings – beautiful – and I see the wagtails but I do not know what song

---

2   In Buddhism, dharma means truth, nature, law, order, duty: the secret of nature which must be understood in order to develop life to the highest possible purpose and benefit.

they sing. I feed the birds every day if I can. I always do my best to listen to their chat.

I have been doing yogic breaths each night for one or two hours. Very helpful. I'm only able to get any yoga done at the weekends as the weeks are so busy and taken up with routine. Every spare moment I get I'm in meditation. I'm doing about four hours of meditation a day. I give myself some time to play the guitar and watch TV. I still daydream far too much, whatever this 'I' is that does it. The choir has begun again. Dawn and Isobel have come back to do another show with us. We are putting on a concert in seven weeks.

With each day that passes my fear of death gets less. And although fear comes each day at some point, I am for the first time in my life facing up to this false demon. I'm enjoying the practice, my friend, I am enjoying the path; as difficult as it does get at times, it really is the only worthwhile thing to do with one's life.

I can honestly say that my life has been transformed into something worthwhile. I may not be able to say on my deathbed that my life was a complete success but I can say that it was not a waste. That is important.

Forever your friend,
   Max

....

Dear friend Max,

Your disciplined use of your time – four hours meditating each day plus time for yoga at the weekend – is admirable. Lovely that the choir has started again but even more lovely that you can truly say that your life has not been a waste of time and that you are experiencing genuine happiness in the practice.

Your experience of a need for nothing at all says so much to me. Not that I have had that experience – except perhaps a superficial glimpse – but it seems so essential to our practice because as long as we think we need anything, whatever it may be, we are still full of our own ego's cravings and opinions. Sometimes when people ask me what meditation is about, I can only think of saying 'emptying yourself'. It seems to me that that is precisely what it is about.

How wonderful to feel that sense of liberation, but I can understand the fear as well, as it *is* a step into the unknown. I like your term 'an alarming success'. Sometimes it is important to look back, especially at times when it feels as though we have not advanced at all, and see how in fact we have changed. Imperceptibly, without manoeuvring it ourselves, somehow it just happens. It is amazing that you have got so far with so very little help and never a constant teacher at your side. I know you read a lot but books aren't the same as a person.

I sometimes feel, too, as though I will never escape from my overly judgemental and opinionated mind. It is so difficult to let go and let things be as they are. Appreciate the moment and not be half somewhere else or wishing things were different – and especially that must be difficult in prison.

It is Pentecost (Whitsunday) today. I love it as I really truly do believe in the power of the Holy Spirit – or whatever you like to call it.

May you feel that power within you, dear friend. You are such a wonderful companion along the way,

Wendy

....

Dear Wendy,

It's 10 a.m. on a wet day, a very wet day. I am sitting outside the cell trying to write with all the craziness going on around me. As I sit here and hear the conversations I can't help but have compassion, as I realise how lost we are and how no-one has anything constructive to say.

Over the past few weeks I have been going through some different understandings. My view of the world is really changing, even the way that I see others. Some of the old traits are still there but something does seem to be coming to the surface.

Maybe I should not be too surprised by this for over the last nine years of practice there has been a lot of work put in, so at some point fruit must appear. The main kernel of the practice these days is, of course, to develop the heart; but I am also trying to work with transcending discrimination and non-discrimination, transcending attachment and indifference. This is a very important practice.

I seem to have less fears in many areas of life, including death. Anxiety still arises, but that is a chemical imbalance and a habitual process.

I love your description of opening yourself to be a channel of love and peace. I so agree. This *is* the only way to a productive life. Only love, no matter what is going on around you. I realise that if that can be made manifest at all times, then one has mastered one's life, that, and of course, mastered all fears.

Even though this place is a cacophony, it is in many ways a great opportunity. This is my place of practice, my monastery, and I must learn to embrace it fully. If I can do this, then I will have learnt so much. Simply put, I must use this time to full advantage.

As always, I hope this finds you in good spirits. Much love,
      Your friend Max

....

Dear friend Max,

I went to a film called *Boyhood* yesterday, and the boy in it points out to his girlfriend how they all live life through a screen rather than experiencing things as they are around them. The boy was surrounded by adults who spent their whole time telling him what to do, even though they themselves had made messes of their own lives. I think meditation has greatly reduced my temptation to do that – or maybe I now simply lack the energy to try to control what other people do, or maybe I know now that giving advice never changes people in any case!

You talk about how your view of the world is really changing. I think practising meditation brings with it a real change in ourselves which we usually don't notice until something happens which makes us realise that we are reacting in a different way to people or events, or perhaps want different things in life from those we have previously wanted.

You say that you have become less anxious about many things, including the thought of dying. I think that that is the experience of most people who practise serious meditation. It is certainly the case with me, though this doesn't mean that I am never anxious, and often about ridiculous things.

Glenochil *is* your monastery, as one's monastery has to be wherever one is; but my heart is filled with so much joy and admiration when you say that you accept that that is where your practice must take place and that you must use the opportunity of your time there to full advantage. You motivate me to put more time and effort into following this way. Here I am with much more congenial surroundings: am I making the most of them?

Let's keep going Max, encouraging each other along the way. Tramp, tramp!
Wendy

....

Dear Wendy,

Keeping a good heart is the most important thing for me, though it is not always easy by any means. Things are more compounded here, so it is all too easy to be pulled into something which doesn't have any bearing on your life. Once at lunch time, a 30-year-old man was going to smash a 40-year-old man's face in because he didn't get enough chips at the hot plate. War was narrowly avoided by the diplomatic efforts of a third man with a sachet of tomato sauce. He convinced the aggrieved party that though he did have fewer chips, he now had the added pleasure of covering them in sauce to make a chip sandwich. Happy with that, the aggressor backed down, his pride intact.

What I always try to keep in mind is the story of the monk who escaped to India after 16 years of being held by the Chinese.

The Dalai Lama asked him: 'During your imprisonment, were you ever afraid?' He said, only once was he frightened, when he thought he might lose his compassion for the Chinese.

When our fear touches someone's pain it becomes pity; when our love touches someone's pain it becomes compassion. We cannot change the world by feeling sorry for it but we can change the world within ourselves, and then we will be changing the world. For me this can only be done through the act of meditation. If we allow our meditation to be part of our daily life and allow our daily life to be part of meditation, then something special will come up, which is not easy to put into words. I like to say that one gains the ability always to do, to think and to say the right thing. Each time you sit down to meditate, whether you are aware of it or not you are showing more LOVE to the universe and all the things within it than you could possibly imagine. In fact, if you felt the power of that love you would likely pass out. That is why we always get things slowly in our practice.

Just so you know, I had an awful time of hatred towards the guards for two days a short time back. I really struggled. Was it the guards' ways that caused my hatred? Absolutely not. It was my reluctance to let go.

Much love to you dear Wendy. Always and ever your friend,
Max

....

Dear friend Max,

The wisest among you must be the best trained people in conflict resolution in the world. How important that man who offered the sauce was, especially as he probably was looking forward to eating it himself.

I love what you write about pity – I have never before thought of it being based on fear. It is so different from compassion, which doesn't have that sense of superiority that pity does. Compassion is a feeling of solidarity between equals. It is a privilege to be able to help other people, but is draining if you don't quite manage

173

to forget yourself enough! That we cannot change the world by feeling sorry for it but only by transforming ourselves is such a wonderful thing to say. All this fills me with a sense of 'all things are possible', if only we can forget ourselves. Thank you with all my heart for writing all this to me.

I do always know you are sitting with me and I with you. I often think you are a lamp along my way, sometimes ahead, sometimes alongside me, flickering or steady but always alight.

With love as always,
Wendy

....

Dear Wendy,

I want to tell you something interesting. I had finished my work for the day and started to talk to the Buddha in my head: 'You know, Buddha, you are breaking my heart. Why is this such a difficult thing? Why do I always feel as though I was swimming upstream?' At that point a young woman who is one of the civilian workers came by. She turned to tell me that she had put in the stores order and that the only thing she couldn't get for me were small gloves. I said, 'That's all right as they are only for me because I have got small hands.' She said, 'So do I, Max,' and as she walked away, she said, 'See, you're not alone Max, you're not alone.' To me it felt like a message by proxy from the universe. I was made up by it, completely stoked. I should really learn to focus on such things with more faith.

My calendar this month says: 'When I am inspired by the desire to practise and transform my suffering, the mind of the moment is very beautiful. Sometimes we call it the mind of love. It is because of love that we wish to practise.'

I say it out loud to myself each day to remind myself just how much the practice is about everyone. Although when I sit I do so for my illusory self, at a much deeper level I know that I do what I do for the benefit of all sentient beings. After all, what else is there?

Thanks for the lovely photo you took of the geese. I hope the retreat went well and that also you didn't find it too painful to sit for long periods. Though the benefits of painful sitting are huge. It is when we sit through pain till we can't take any more that we then reach a point in our practice in which we begin to understand that pain is not you and you are not pain.

The turnaround experienced through our meditation is simply not possible to understand with the human mind. That's why it is called letting go. It takes courage to continue sitting, but what else is there? Back to the old ways or follow on the way. If you ask any mountaineer who has climbed the highest peaks on the planet, does it get easier the further up you go, he or she will tell you that it gets more challenging the further up they go, right to the very top. Our practice is no different.

I have no idea why I sit any more. I do recall a few years back when I was sitting because I wanted to get nice experiences. I wanted to be a better person. That was always something I wanted from my practice. Even to be a Buddha. These days the reason why I sit is because it makes sense to do so. And you should know that 175 sometimes I get concerned about sitting because I don't know what will come up, but I won't let even that stop me...

I have to face up to the possibility that I might have to spend the rest of my days in prison. And if that is the way it turns out, then I will embrace it as part of my life's tapestry.

And with that I will say good night. Yours ever,
    Max

....

Being with the Blues

The blues might be anything from being a bit low in spirits, to long-standing depression, to sudden news knocking you for six, like a letter from your partner or spouse telling you it's over. Meditation really can make a difference – both as prevention and as part of a range of things that you do to try to alleviate depression, including exercise (yoga or otherwise) and anti-depressants. As we see in various letters, people do meditate while taking anti-depressants: it's not one or the other. Please realise, too, that reducing your medication is not a sign that you are 'good' at meditation: you have to use the right means at the right time to work on getting yourself out of your slump.

Bob, HMP Coldingley

Dear Kate,

I have fallen into one of my deep, dark, unrelenting depressions.
And I haven't the faintest idea why. I just woke up one day
depressed it seemed, and it's not budging. I'm not eating as much,
I've missed gym sessions and lie in bed all day. I suppose I've had
a lot to deal with lately, what with my brother's death and all, but
I can't find any other reason for it. Looking forward to hearing
from you.

Yours sincerely,
    Bob

....

Dear Bob,

I'm always happy when I know there is a letter from you, but I'm
sorry to hear that you are feeling depressed. You are exactly right
about depression – it seems to just arrive, like a cold – only a cold
usually goes away after a week or two, and depression can hang
around. It is at least partly a chemical imbalance in the brain –
when we don't have enough serotonin, we feel low. And it seems
that some people are better at producing this chemical than others,
so it's maybe partly genetic.

It is possible to increase the serotonin in the brain, by eating,
and by exercise, and by trying to get enough daylight (this might
be difficult for you to do). But the problem with feeling depressed
is that the thought of doing anything positive seems pointless, and
like it's too much effort. I have certainly felt this way at times,
and I guess that must be how you are feeling now.

If you can, just do one small thing each day that might help
you feel better. Maybe a bit of exercise or yoga – but only a bit;
don't make plans to do a lot, and then feel depressed because you
didn't manage it. So just to stand up straight in the mountain pose
and notice your breathing – this is a deep practice, and maybe one
that you can do.

Sometimes when I do yoga, and particularly if I'm feeling low or lazy, I start with something really easy, like the mountain. Then I wait and let the body choose the next pose, which might be lying down, or maybe lifting the arms into the air with the in-breath, lowering them with the out-breath. By letting the body choose, it's possible to let go of the notion that I 'have' to do anything in particular, and I find this really useful.

The other thing I am practising these days, when I begin yoga or meditation, or when the mind has wandered off, or when I go to sleep, is four simple breaths with these words silently in mind:

In......out

Deep......slow

Calm......ease

Smile......release

I find this really helps me to come into the present and get free of my busy mind.

I'm sure I've said all this to you before, Bob, but the other thing that can really help depression is meditation. It changes the way the brain works, so that we start to feel better. There is a lot of complicated science to support this now, but the basic fact is that, strange as it seems, sitting still and being in the present moment is actually more effective to prevent depression than taking medication.

Again, sometimes the idea of 'doing' meditation is too much to think about. In Japan, they call meditation *zazen*, which means 'just sitting'. I like this, because we can all just sit. No matter how terrible you feel, you can just sit. This is enough. There is something about sitting up that makes us feel less overwhelmed, and by beginning to have physical equilibrium, it's possible to have mental/emotional equilibrium as well – at least, this is my experience. Really all of this is just an experiment – try it, and see how it is for you.

Take care of yourself Bob. Your friend,
   Kate

....

Mark, HMP Albany

Dear Sir or Madam,

Reading books such as yours is enlightening, but I find myself making the same stupid mistakes, almost like I'm on a conveyor belt. I want to change and be educated in my faulty ways.

I'm a lifer prisoner with a 15-year tariff for murder, which has haunted me for the past eight years. I suffer with depression, but my medication does nothing to help lessen my grief. Something seems to have this hold on my being, like it's too painful to confront one's self. I find it very hard to give myself credit for anything I do.

I have a friend here, and we both enjoy yoga and have tried to start a class up. We try to practise two or three times a week. I do it in my cell too, which helps with my anxieties. If you have any information on dealing with anxiety and depression I would be grateful.

Yours faithfully,
Mark

....

Dear Mark,

Your desire to move on from your situation is a huge inspiration. You mention you find yourself making the same mistakes and see the same problems repeating. You are not alone in this, Mark, and breaking out of such cycles can be a long task. However, you are aware of this and that's the first stage.

Beyond this, it may be worth realising what happens whilst we meditate, or whilst we focus the mind upon the body during asana practice. Thoughts arise in our minds, and initially we usually follow these thoughts, which lead us away from the present moment. It can take some effort to regain our centredness and focus the mind back on our breathing. Again, more thoughts arise in the mind, and we lose our focus, and have to return to

181

the breath once more. Have you had yoga or meditation sessions where this continually happens? I certainly have. This is just like the problems you mentioned, where they occur over and over. It is worth trying to return to your breathing as soon as you become aware of such thoughts. This need not be just in a yoga or meditation session, but any time you find yourself disturbed by the busy mind. These disturbing thoughts eventually subside, but it takes patience.

You mention how difficult it is 'to confront one's self'. Perhaps it would be easier not to confront, but simply to accept the self. You may find that the self you are now is very different to the one from years ago. The old self simply does not exist any more. I only know you from this current letter, and honesty, courage, and openness shine out from your words. There would seem to be little reason to confront such qualities, only to wholeheartedly accept them.

Love,
Jason

....

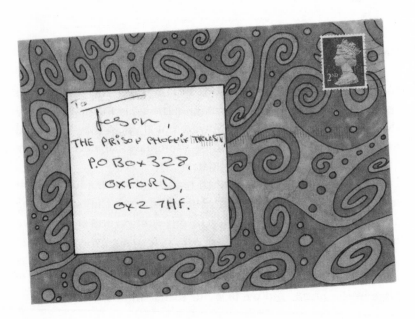

Dear Jason,

Your words brought much comfort. For as long as I can remember, friends, family, prison officers have all at some point tried to help me see the good in me that I've found hard to see or acknowledge. But your letter has opened my mind, eyes and heart. All the books I've read on spirituality have suddenly started making sense. I can't explain what I feel, I just know that a sense of calm has drowned out some of the ignorance and anger that's blinded me for so long.

My life has been filled with violence and suffering that I now know came from my own doing mostly. I knew in my heart that I would one day overcome such painful experiences. Even when I've been at rock bottom, survival was my key. Maybe it's a stubborn streak that refuses to bow down in the face of adversity, or maybe it is just my spirit that's shining through?

Now for the confusing side of me. I know only too well that if I continue to inflict myself with mental torture by not forgiving myself for my crimes, I will never be able to be in peace.

I first experienced prison at 16, when life was, let's just say, very out of focus. I spent much time in and out from then to the age of 26, when I was sentenced to life for the murder. Me and my partner were dependent on heroin then. You have probably heard this a million times, but I truly regret, and wish I could turn back the clock.

Over the years I've felt the wrath of the system but I've come to realise that my biggest battles are internal, deeply rooted in my soul. You see, I don't hate the guards or people around me. At times of despair, I cannot bring myself to even check my reflection in the mirror.

Thank you for your time and kindness. Your friend,
   Mark
....

Dear Mark,

I understand your poignant thought that you cannot turn the clock back. This is a profound truth for us all, and choosing our own path and bearing the consequences is a responsibility none of us can avoid.

But we can choose how we view the past. To decide that an action is simply right or wrong inevitably leads to elation or guilt. Such thoughts can arise and recede in our minds for many years. If we choose only to classify an action as 'wrong', we gain yet another load to carry on our shoulders.

Perhaps it is helpful also to view actions as appropriate or inappropriate. We don't have to carry this burden of 'wrong', but instead we live with the consequences and accept them as part of our life. Maybe this is where the key to putting the past behind us lies: by wholeheartedly accepting that we have made inappropriate choices, we become free to choose another path.

Your 'stubborn streak' that refuses to bow down in the face of adversity could be seen to be a great quality, especially where it manifests as resolution and determination. However, most people with such resolute natures are usually well aware of a more accepting side to their character. Sometimes acceptance is misunderstood as a weaker quality: passivity. So determination changes to stubbornness. In the practice of yoga and meditation, both sides are important and act as a balance. A sense of resolution can give courage to face up to our inner selves, and acceptance can allow us to be watchful but not interfering. Many creatures have this balance. They can sit still and watch for a long time, then move swiftly and precisely, before returning to stillness once again.

Do you find in prison that both these qualities are required? To be able to watch and not to interfere, but also to be willing to face up to unexpected difficulties could be very useful. You can be certain these qualities will be balanced and controlled by your yoga practice.

184   It is great knowing you. Love,
     Jason

Dear Jason,

Since our last correspondence I've found myself in a difficult position. For some time I have been wanting to attend the psychodrama group therapy. My first application was unsuccessful due to not being here long enough and difficulty in settling into the therapy routine of things. Over the last six months I feel I have put myself forward in many difficult areas and learnt so much about myself and other people. So I was quite positive, thinking that all should be fine for me to apply a second time and be successful. But once again I've been told that I am not ready and that I have to work on my anger.

I'm still very angry inside, but I also understand the impact of my offence and issues that other people will have to deal with. I am hurting inside and it's like I am not being allowed to try and heal and do good for my lost son. These feelings and emotions take me back to that dreaded day in hospital when I was told of the loss of my son. I knew I was responsible, and felt completely powerless to help in any way whatsoever. I thought this particular prison could give me the chance to learn, heal and repair, but now I've a head of broken glass and mixed messages once again.

My impulse is to shout and scream and even run away from this prison, but I know that it will only haunt me somewhere else. It's like standing on hot coals trying to find that spot that might give a little solace and comfort, but you look around and there is no island to give hope. You need huge strength to deal with this. It's like a continuous irritation – so tedious and so longing to be scratched or put to rest.

Still, I am enjoying my yoga class and learning new ways and things about myself and the true essence and spirit of yoga. Rosita is a good teacher. This morning I practised for 90 minutes and felt really free and alive afterwards. My meditation is going fine also. I'm hoping to receive my cushion and mat soon.

Take care, my good spiritual friend. Peace always,
   Mark

Dear Mark,

You mention not being able to attend psychodrama. Can you discuss your thoughts with someone at the prison? I don't know, only you can know, but perhaps you are simply not meant to attend the psychodrama group at this time. Perhaps it is best to take this no further, and simply to re-apply next time with an open mind. Sometimes situations are hard to accept, but provide the best possible outcome for everyone. This might be one of those times. If you can, try not to trace the reasons back to your original offence: this may just make you suffer and feel apart from things and other people. I am sure you agree that you have moved on from those dark times, and have become a very different and special person as a result.

To me, inner strength is available to anyone at any time, enabling us to remain peaceful and consistent during difficult situations. The feeling of courage seems slightly different, in that it enables us to face up and react to situations in an appropriate way, which is sometimes purely inward. It is important to let the courage grow from inner strength. Perhaps you have noticed this during periods of silence, when all situations are seen as transitional and temporary. During these moments of stillness, the best way to accept the present situation arises quite naturally.

Thanks again for writing, Mark. It would be great to be able to provide you with an answer which would resolve these feelings, but the stillness and silence inside yourself will do a better job than that.

With best wishes,
    Jason
....

Dear Jason,

I'm glad to let you know that I am now allowed to move back to B Cat conditions with the objective of going to a C Cat. I am still feeling rather vulnerable due to not being able to trust the system, as I've been let down by them so many times in the past. For me, trust is something none of us can live without really, so we take a risk whether it is with friends, family, etc. But I go wrong in believing that all will be okay. Am I letting myself in for upset here by doing so? We have to take a chance, don't we? Maybe it all comes down to how one deals with the knocks and bangs that enables them to move forwards.

Yours,
    Mark

....

Dear Mark,

You are right that trust is a fundamental quality, and at times this can be hard to find, especially when living in an overcrowded prison system. It could drive a person mad trying to think their way through such a complex situation.

Perhaps it is better to trust in smaller things. We can trust in our breathing, and the way this revolves around the present moment. The breath is with us wherever we find ourselves, and if we can trust in this, the most appropriate action is free to come naturally. Everything is in safe hands.

Your transfer to a different prison will come at the right time, and you are right to believe that not only will things be okay, but things *are* okay. You must feel buffeted and bashed with all the changes and transfers you have been through in the prison system. But just like a ship negotiating a stormy sea, you keep forging ahead.

I am certain there is something good looking after you through these times, Mark.

With peace and good wishes,
    Jason

....

Dear Jason,

For some time now I've been making a true effort in my meditation practice. This practice doesn't just consist of sitting but being aware of everyday things that we all at times are guilty of ignoring or taking for granted. For instance, over time I've noticed that I need to work on the little things that evoke my negative emotions. So I've decided to hand in my television set. Since doing this I am now much more aware of the noise levels and other people's habits, probably more so than they are themselves.

I've been doing a lot of reading and practising and notice that I have become quite sensitive and somewhat fragile in some ways, like with my emotions. I feel emotionally weaker than normal, but on the other hand I am working on coping and dealing with things that annoy me. Is this emotional issue coming forwards now that I've chosen to uncover it and reveal it to myself? Could this be me trying to reveal the real me? I try so hard to face my inner fears and work on my weaknesses but sometimes it all gets a little too much and then I end up being harsh with myself for making a slight mistake, whether that's being abrupt to someone or letting myself down in some other ways.

Best wishes
 Mark

....

Dear Mark,

We only recommend concentration upon the breath. Some forms of meditation feature visualisations, but simply focusing on the breath is a simple practice that is safe and very effective. Many people continue with this method all their life. There are times where emotions become strong, and that is perfectly okay. Your experience and practice will help you to be with your emotions without needing to change them.

Perhaps you remember Michael, who you helped at Long Lartin. He writes to me still and I remember how highly he thought of you. Michael now practises regularly, and like the rest of us is trying to find the best way forwards.

You are quite an inspiration to others, Mark. Just keep responding, and all you need will be with you.

With peace,
  Jason

....

Dear Jason,

Why is it that things always sound and seem much clearer inside our heads but at times, when it comes to speaking, writing or any other action that helps to express oneself, it never seems to flow or come out how we truly expect? Maybe that's just it: expectations.

Could it all truly be this simple? If so, then I'm going to stop or at least try to not question or doubt things so often. Letting be, I feel, has helped me to understand my thoughts and cope with my anxieties and depression over time.

My past sins have been many, and shame and guilt has stopped me from giving myself permission to really enjoy life, to feel happy, to let myself go without worrying how I might look to other people. My life has been controlled by man-made restraints and imposed rules and regulations, but now I choose to find the lock and the key within me to make things better – and I mean better for all. I no longer wish to sit under that great shadow of the albatross.

Take care my friend,
  Mark

....

Dear Mark,

Perhaps so many thoughts have been let go, all there is left is to express yourself with no thought of what others think or feel. This could be the time to express feelings before thinking. For instance, on my desk are beautiful flowers: Yellow! I open the window and the cold air comes in: Chilly! I sit still and feel distracted: Busy mind! All these feelings coming and going: what else can there be?

It would be interesting to know how your current choices are making you feel about others – do you feel closer or more apart?

I admire your dedication to following this path. It cannot be easy feeling free inside, yet restricted in a prison. Maybe this seeming contradiction can provide the energy to break free of concepts and boundaries.

Our thoughts are with you always,
  Jason

....

Dear Jason,

If my feelings are getting out of control I talk to myself and give a gentle reminder to put pride on the shelf and then the inner work of honesty and wisdom comes forth. This can be in the form of meditation, reading, writing or even prayer to others – love and kindness. If I can say a prayer for someone who may have wronged me then I am left feeling calm and at ease, not full of anger. It has taken many, many frustrations and much suffering to get to where I am today within my spiritual quest of self. Even our spiritual strength is tested to breaking point and beyond.

I now constantly try to stay awake by being honest with myself and practise by avoiding all the pitfalls of old. A hurdle that I am working on at present is guilt and not beating myself up constantly because it affects my every action. Learning to accept and forgive myself for my past sins hasn't been easy but I now understand the importance of doing so. I am much more at ease now and don't feel so bad for having a good day or a smile upon my face.

Thank you for your kind words and wisdom.

Your friend,
  Mark

....

Dear Mark,

Your letter shows how your practice manages to lift you, even though you still feel impatient and frustrated. There reaches a stage where we cannot fail to make progress towards wholeness. No matter how frustrating life becomes, or how many times we repeat the same habits, something deep inside is being healed. We may not be aware of the process, but every now and again a crack appears and we see a glimpse of something wonderful inside. The way you write so lucidly about your innermost feelings shows you know this truth.

It is beautiful that you find time to think of others and offer a prayer of love and kindness. Are there other ways you show your kindness to others? Maybe this is the way forward – simply to help those around you to find peace within themselves. It is not by accident that you are surrounded by people who feel broken and lonely: as you know, other prisoners have written to us, inspired by your calmness and strength.

In peace and friendship,
Jason

....

Dean, HMP Swinfen Hall

Dear PPT,

I've read your books and would be interested to learn some more. I have found the practices and breathing techniques helpful during my cell time at night. After about two weeks I started to feel a difference and others have noticed too.

I felt an awakening of something inside and a greater understanding of who I am through quietening the mind. It's made me feel happier and the days are flying by. I used to suffer from depression. I still do from time to time as I suppose we all do. But generally my spirits are lifted. The only trouble I'm finding with the practices is that when I get the odd day where I feel low, I find it hard to motivate myself with my sitting as my mind gets restless. Any tips or advice on how to keep on track when things aren't going great?

Yours sincerely,
Dean

....

Dear Dean,

Sometimes it is hard to get motivated to sit when you feel low. First of all please know that none of us find it easy. The first step is recognising that you are actually feeling low. Whilst sitting, focus upon your breathing, and know that feeling this way is totally acceptable. It is a common misunderstanding that those who regularly practise yoga and meditation do not ever feel low or depressed (or all the other emotions of our human nature). The difference is to recognise feelings and know that they will arise and recede again. Our true home is in the silence that these thoughts emanate from, and you have already awakened to this state of acceptance and stillness in your practice. When you are feeling low (or angry, jealous, victimised or lonely) just accept yourself in this state just as you are. Then when you bring your attention to the breath, pour all of your feelings into the out-breath and just let the in-breath wash in. This continual 'washing' in meditation helps you feel better.

With good wishes for your meditation and all the discoveries it is bringing you,
    Jason

If I miss one day's practice, I notice it.

If I miss two days' practice, the critics notice it.

If I miss three days' practice, the public notice it.

Franz Liszt, Hungarian composer
and pianist, 1811–1886

Geoff, HMP High Down

Like so many people in prison, Geoff has had many ups and downs. We start his exchange with Kate, who he's been writing to since 2008, at a point when he is especially low.

Dear Kate,

Things have gotten progressively worse since our last contact, in all areas of my life, which has ended with me being transferred to this B Cat from a C Cat, much to my dismay. It started years ago when I was sent to a secure hospital and the doctor there took it upon himself to not treat me with the recommended drug I needed and I became progressively ill when I was taken off my medication. I then took ill with a fungal virus, which I think turned into pneumonia. It was only when I filed for a legal review that I was returned to HMP Long Lartin, untreated after 12 months for nothing but my blood pressure.

The stomach problems from my time in the secure hospital were never diagnosed or treated except for when I was diagnosed with a hiatus hernia in 2014, although I've persistently complained of stomach pain, sleeplessness and feelings of anxiety. Last October I became very, very unwell. I woke up vomiting and over the next few days got progressively sicker. It took two weeks to see a doctor. I had ruptured my hiatus hernia and developed chronic bowel disorder. Crazily, I soldiered on, going to work when I could and going to education to do my drug counselling course. If I'd known bed rest was a requirement for recovery I'd have asked the doctor for time off immediately.

I had to do all the research for the condition, ask for the right medication and ask for hospital referrals. As soon as I asked for a couple of weeks off work, I was transferred on the pretence I was mentally ill, all while being hassled and harassed by officers and governors over minor trivial matters. The insinuation that I am mentally ill is ridiculous.

When I called for medical assistance four times one day as I was in extreme pain and could taste blood, nobody came even though Oscar 2 emergency was activated. I did not have a kettle, mirror or television for three weeks even though I was paying for a television. There is no window in my cell to shut and everything is in a state of disrepair. There is hardly any wing association, and the exercise yard is like a rubbish dump. Also I'm having trouble with my left leg. I'm not sure if it's a nerve problem or I have a thrombosis. It's impossible to talk to staff here at any level. Stupidity and sadism seem to be the order of the day.

Nearly all of my outside relationships have collapsed. Mostly family, some friends. I can only count my mother and two friends as support now. I'm still very, very unwell, and keep thinking I may die of cancer or this bloody thing that's wrong with my leg.

Apart from writing letters, I do not know what to do. It seems everything is to chance, and as the old saying goes 'in the hands of the gods'.

Love, respect and peace,
Geoff

....

Dear Geoff,

I have been thinking of you these past months, so it is good to hear from you, even though things are clearly very difficult. I am so, so sorry. It seems everything is a muddle – being transferred to a different prison and trying to get someone to take your health issues seriously. The main thing that I think would help is to have someone there who can listen to you and take your health concerns seriously. If you do have a ruptured hiatus hernia, this may be serious, and you need proper medical attention. Do you have a probation officer there? If not, perhaps go to the chaplain. Also, if you can put your name down for counselling, you will get someone who knows who you are and who cares for you. And obviously you need to see a doctor. Keep asking.

You were doing well and with good support at your previous prison, so it is painful to hear that everything has fallen apart since then. No wonder you feel frustrated and angry. And yet, in the absence of outer support, you need to find your inner resources. I say this, Geoff, because I know that you can do this. First, take a cool view and work out if you were more stable and positive when you were on your medication. If so, then at least while you are moving through these difficult times, think about seeing a doctor and just having a stabilising dose. When we are in pain, sometimes we need extra help.

The other thing: when there is nowhere else to turn, we can get in touch with that deeper part of our selves. When you hit rock bottom and there is no way out, that is the time to turn towards meditation. I know you feel resistant, but resistance is just part of the human condition. Acknowledge it, and don't let it imprison you. 'I may not feel much like doing anything, but I am going to do it anyway.' Just to feel, to listen to your breathing, is to turn towards the miraculous. When there is no-one else to heal us, then we have to find the strength to begin to heal ourselves. I know you have the capacity and the wisdom to do this. And I know you are worth it. The place you are in now will not last forever, so somehow you need to find the strength to endure until change occurs. The problem with anger is that it takes up a lot of energy, and right now, you need to use the energy you have to look after yourself with immense kindness. And the kindest thing that we do, both for ourselves and for the suffering of the world, is to meditate.

With love,
    Kate

....

Dear Kate,

It seems that the worst things in life seem to happen to me, no matter how hard I try, or how often I try to get help. I've done nothing but suffer since October, I've come to this prison and things got increasingly worse. My family have abandoned me, and my friends. I can hardly eat. I'm never going to get proper healthcare I think. I've no future now, no health, no family, no friends. I have been systematically destroyed by the prison system.

Love,
Geoff

....

Dear Geoff,

It makes me sad and upset that you are going through such difficult times. If I could trade places with you, I would.

I went to see a very moving exhibition of a Chinese protest artist, Ai Wei Wei, last December in London. He is critical of the Chinese government, and they really don't like that in China. So one time, when he was about to fly to Taiwan, they arrested him at the airport and put him into detention for 81 days. He was in a cell that was about eight by ten feet. And the whole time he was in there, while he slept, while he ate, while he sat on the loo, while he showered, there were two prison officers in there with him, not allowed to be more than 80 centimetres away from him. They were not allowed to speak to him (other than interrogations). So he was watched 24/7 for 81 days. I guess they were trying to drive him mad. But Ai Wei Wei is so strong, so unsinkable, that he just survived it, I think by taking in every detail of what was happening. Because afterwards, when he got out, he made a piece of art that took up a huge gallery room. They were six boxes, each half the real size of his cell, with a model of him and the two prison guards, standing over him while he slept, while he ate, while he showered. By transforming it into art, he survived.

The thing is, from our point of view, he had done nothing wrong. I was thinking about this: I think it is a universal human experience – we get accused of doing something, and then we get punished. This must happen to every child, I think, to every person who has been abused. A sense of outrage and anger arises. But it's important not to be trapped. The anger makes us ill. So if I can't 'stomach' what is happening to me, that anger can turn inwards and eat away at me.

197

Here is another story. It is one that stays with me, because the person in it does something that I probably couldn't do. It goes like this:

There was a teenage girl living with her parents in a small village in Japan, a long time ago. The girl became pregnant. The parents were outraged, and demanded to know who the father was. The girl, under much pressure, eventually told them that it was the local priest. The parents went to the priest, and accused him of getting their daughter pregnant. They gave him the baby, and told him he had to look after it. All the priest said was, 'Is that so?'

So the priest took in the child, and looked after it as best he could. The priest was, of course, disgraced, and no-one brought him donations any more, so life was very hard. Eventually, the young girl, watching this situation, couldn't stand it any longer. She confessed that the priest was not the father of the child – that it had been an itinerant labourer. The parents again went to the priest, and begged his forgiveness, and told him they were taking the child back home. All the priest said was, 'Is that so?'

It's remarkable that the priest does not go down the path of moral outrage. He knows he is not the father of the child, but he also knows that the parents will not believe him, whatever he says. So he just looks after the child, so that it will not suffer.

Your situation is, of course, different. It is hard to swallow injustice, especially when there is no way to make your voice heard. I know things can go wrong in an unsupported environment. But I am going to say something to you, and I know I have said it before: which is to turn your mind towards understanding, and compassion. Obviously you need to offer kindness towards yourself, through yoga, through finding ways of moving the mind out of its habit energy of anger. And now the hard part: to offer kindness to those who have hurt or accused you, to realise that they are suffering too. Can you do this? It is not easy. Start with yourself: *May I be safe and well...* Geoff, I know that right now you do not feel safe or well. I really know that. But just to turn the mind to a different path means it not falling into the rut of outrage.

It may not seem like much, but just to listen to your breath, to feel the palm of your hand, to ground the soles of your feet on the floor. These small things can be calming, even healing.

I know you have hit rock bottom. I know things seem utterly hopeless. When every other option is exhausted, that is the moment to give up and just sit. This just sitting is the beginning and the meaning of meditation. When I have been deeply depressed, it is the only thing that helped me. I really pray that it will help you too.

I am sending you a postcard by an artist from Tobago. Can you feel the warmth of the sun coming from it?

Love,
   Kate

....

Out of the Madness

'I planted so much hate and anger in my early years. Now it's time to plant love for my fellow humans,' said someone who had spent a long time using drugs. He faced serious trials extracting himself from the culture and chaotic life that often goes with addiction – 'the madness' as he called it. With support from his prison's RAPt unit he started to work on his addiction. He started meditating too. After practising twice a day for eight months, he said he was finally able to look himself in the eye and smile.

Another friend inside had the madness of withdrawal and of reducing his methadone. When medical staff refused his script one day, he felt even more vulnerable than usual. Returning to his single cell, feeling desperate and worried about what he might do to himself, he found a letter waiting from the person he writes to at the PPT. After reading it, he felt like trying to get a handle on things, so he sat down on the edge of his bed and did the breathing exercises he had learned in recent weeks. 'Afterwards I could see my insecurities and emotions for what they are,' he wrote. So he started doing it every morning again, which he said helped with the physical pain of withdrawal, and with his anxiety.

Someone else who writes to us said, 'Meditation has helped me no end with my heroin addiction. I was terrified to come off the methadone, but eight weeks clean, and I'm a human being again, but only with the comfort of my meditation.'

For other people, life feels out of control because they've seen extreme violence or experienced abuse and neglect earlier in their lives. Yet even for the very powerful symptoms of post-traumatic stress disorder that some people experience, meditation and yoga can help. One ex-serviceman wrote that meditation was helping to ease the debilitating flashbacks which had landed him in jail in the first place, and was helping him to become the person he used to be.

There are other kinds of impossible situations that we can get ourselves into, like the one Donna describes in her letters, or the bullying and temptation of drugs that surrounds Nick. You may feel that your version of the madness is unique. But know you're not alone in wanting to find a way out. Know too that sometimes, the greater the struggle is, the greater the peace that comes through sticking at it.

Denise

Throughout my life I always took things to the limit. When I used heroin I did it with complete commitment: I had a full, long-lasting relationship with the drug. I also used cocaine, amphetamines, cannabis and lots of LSD when I was younger.

I had a childhood that was fairly disturbed. My sister went into hospital when I was about two years old. I was left at a hardware shop each day whilst my mother visited my sister in hospital. At an early age I began suffering from insecurity and fears of abandonment. I was sexually abused by a man who lived up the street when I was about eight, and when I was 17, I became pregnant. My mother forced me to go into a Catholic home for unmarried mothers and have my child adopted. Soon after, I started using drugs. I married for a month – another drug user – and I just drifted.

I found my teacher (or my teacher found me) in 1974, and I got involved in the practice of yoga because of my friends and for a feeling of belonging. It was only many years later that I started to fully accept the gift that I had been given; then the real changes began to happen.

I received a four-year sentence for supplying heroin, and when I went into prison – about 1985 – I started my practice again. I was aware of Ram Dass and his prison ashram projects and I wrote to the Prison Phoenix Trust and received the newsletters. I also had a Buddhist chaplain visiting me, an amazing woman called Diana who really helped me. She had faith in me and was very kind. There was a group of four or five women in Styal prison who would all come together on a Sunday afternoon with Diana. We would have a little food, perhaps read from different spiritual texts. I am still in touch with Diana. She is a great friend.

Prison is a strange time. Women seem to become like children: the officers tend to call us their girls, and there are water fights on the landings, brushing each other's hair in the television room and a great feeling of closeness within the houses in Styal prison. In prison I was in a four-bed dormitory. When I wanted to meditate I would go into the washroom, after the officers had been to check us all at 10 p.m. I awoke before they came to wake us because I wanted to wake myself up. At first other women would try to joke about my meditation, but they soon saw they could not break me by embarrassing me. It was my way of surviving what was a pretty dull existence. I feel what I was doing was respected; the jokes quickly died away.

It is difficult for anyone in prison to be different from the majority. It is easier probably to just try to fit into the nothingness. I did use drugs in prison and, because they were limited in supply, I gained an understanding of how much the use of heroin just once would destabilise me for three or four days. Through meditation I saw the benefits of practice and these outweighed the destabilisation of drugs; I no longer wanted the chaos and inconsistencies.

It's hard to convey what prison does to you and what it means, how one survives the shame of being female and having served a prison sentence, how one can break free through all the labels that would stereotype me as a personality disorder or a classic re-offender.

I knew in prison that although I managed the sentence well, I didn't really want to come back. I was accepted on a residential rehabilitation programme on release. I now work as a Senior Drug Dependency Worker, prescribing methadone, counselling and supporting others. I travel to India each November – habitually! – where I lose my hats: I am no longer the drug counsellor, or the house owner, or the mother or the wife. There, I spend time in meditation, on my own, listening to chanting music, participating in puja,[1] sipping Ganges water, praying, and being a simple human being. I have learned to live my life for me, and from my selfishness I have been able to learn unselfishness.

---

1   In Hinduism, puja is any act of worship. The term is also used by Buddhists, Jains and Sikkhs.

Majid, a secure hospital

I meditate and do yoga, pray five times a day and read the Holy Qur'an. It is a good combination for stressful times, which are frequent when incarcerated. Islam teaches patience, faith, non-judging, non-violence and to help those who need it.

Growing up in a West Yorkshire town, I mixed with various cultures and religions. And when I was sent to New Hall Detention Centre in the 70s (now New Hall Women's Prison), I mixed with all colours and creeds. Later in borstal, I met with some good mates. I'm still in contact with two of them.

I believe Allah was slowly nudging me along. Being a Muslim is as comfortable as a comfy fleece or glove. I feel there must have been a reason for everything, even those awful abusive years in children's homes in the 70s and 80s. I used to really hate those that did those awful things to me and all the other kids, but I've learnt a valuable lesson. Hate does more damage to myself than it did to my perpetrators. I don't hate nowadays.

Meditation and yoga and other ways of self-development are free: not to make full use of them is foolish. Not to try to improve your mind is plain daft. Even if I don't get to use all I have learned, I improved my knowledge, and that's just as important.

I feel that every day is an adventure. You never know how the day will pan out. There are always new things to learn, whether they are good or not so good. When I eventually close my eyes, I know I've done my best – for that day.

Smile or say good morning to someone, even if you don't know them. That smile will cheer the other person up, passing on goodness. Better to be cheerful: others benefit, sometimes without you realising it.

Every day after rising, I do yoga to waken my mind and body, which helps me focus on prayer. I pray and then meditate on my day ahead, sometimes five or ten minutes, sometimes longer. It settles me, and prepares my journey. When I feel overwhelmed with events around me that I cannot control, I return to my cell and meditate. This clears my head, slows my heart rate, gives me a clearer picture. I do yoga asanas several times a day.

I cannot change past events. How can I continue my life journey if I am stuck in the past? Holding onto hurt, pain and rage is not healthy. It causes physical problems in the end. Let the past be part of your life, but don't let the past dictate your life. Sometimes I go in the yard and walk alone, think, breathe and enjoy my time, enjoying nature whatever the weather.

I try to help others who have had similar experiences. This helps them and me. It may not solve their problems, but just helps them to deal with them, accept them and move forward.

Donna

Donna attended a taster yoga and meditation workshop that the Prison Phoenix Trust held in her prison as a first step towards setting up a weekly class there. Her exchanges with Jason explore bullying, labels, compassion and her version of 'the madness' – when the apparent virtue of selflessness can be destructive.

Dear Prison Phoenix Trust,

Thank you for the yoga and meditation class on Friday, as well as your interesting newsletter, a good source of motivation. Reading how inmates challenge their only too familiar triggers of frustration has helped me realise it's not just me: people have the same problems everywhere.

Meditation helps me make sense of my emotions and put things in context. However, I still have trouble with my focus and studies. I fear I am perceived as antisocial, keeping myself to myself. But I do not want to waste my sentence in idle banter. I find it hard to get the balance right between being social and independent study.

I attend chapel fortnightly to meditate, but an arranged session more regularly would benefit a lot of us. Cutbacks mean we can no longer gather in a quiet space for weekly meditation, so I would like to improve meditating on my own in the racket.

I read in your newsletter that we can change our labels easily if we change our environment and activity. It seems like the simplest way to escape a rut. The behaviour we choose can also brand us with a label. Therefore we choose our own labels.

There seems to be a need to identify people by labels. People cannot simply be. I wonder why that is. Like the example of a label peeling off, it is very flimsy and doesn't say a lot about a person's individuality or personality underneath. It's almost as if society needs to put people into categories or sections for it to function. I wonder if this is out of fear – the unknown is a very scary place and some will try to avoid it at all costs. By labelling someone, then we know how to deal with them. This suppresses creativity for both parties. If you want to learn something, then stop looking at the superficial flimsy exterior and begin asking questions about what's underneath. This is true for good and bad people. I've found that, after lifting the label on a few people, quite the opposite was true – a 'nice' label can be completely contradictory of what's going on internally.

You believe labels. It's common to trust them. But how horrified you would be to open something you'd bought in the supermarket only to find it's something other than what you thought!

In the same way we can choose our label at will. Perhaps some people are choosing an unhelpful label for themselves, such as 'bully' or 'hard man', but inside they don't really feel like that. They actually feel quite vulnerable, so they over-compensate, and their label is almost transparent. The fear they inject into others is actually stopping them meeting anyone worthwhile, so they always will be vulnerable until they realise it. Nobody will help until they swap their label for 'open to others'.

Thank you for being a listening ear,
   Donna

....

Dear Donna,

You are right: labels can be misleading and inaccurate. 'Prisoner' is a label, and being labelled 'Prison Officer' can be tough too. You are also right when you say they are often created out of fear. There is a great need for belonging and not being outcast, but really these fears are only created through thinking we are separate. The good thing is that YOU can see through these labels.

Your insight reminds me that we need to be aware of and frequently re-evaluate labels. If we label without realising it, it does not take long before our opinions become set. In our thinking, writing, watching and listening, labels come and go endlessly. You must meet many people in prison who wrongly label themselves. Your ability to see through this is so valuable.

Jason
....

Dear Jason,

I have reached another step in my self-discovery and am a little stuck. I have learnt that we have to be our own guides, be able to control our emotions, be in touch with who we are and not let external factors determine our being. However, since I have understood this, I'm feeling really disillusioned because the world isn't perfect like I'd imagined. There is pain and suffering all around, and there always will be. There's no end to it.

So my dilemma is this: how to get inspired when you're up against something unending? No matter how hard I try, pain will always rear its ugly head. I am seeking compassion within myself to be able to conquer the darkness. With compassion I can help myself and perhaps reach my next level of acceptance. But how is compassion cultivated from a vast nothingness?

Yours sincerely,
Miss Donna
....

Dear Donna,

Where to find inspiration when there is so much suffering in the world? This is a big question, and one that can form the basis for how we choose to act and behave. Just knowing that being alive generates feelings of suffering is an important insight. Oddly enough, it is good you understand this truth so well.

In prison you will see so much suffering, but your letter shows that you see this is not confined to difficult environments. Anywhere in the world people will feel some sort of struggle, and knowing this can provide endless empathy. It is this empathy with suffering which can inspire us to make life a little easier for everyone. No-one can eliminate suffering, but we can simplify, offer kindness and try not to increase the difficulties around us. And then the world becomes an easier place for everyone.

You ask how to cultivate compassion from nothingness, and maybe this is easier if you take 'nothingness' to be exactly the present moment. When we sit in meditation, focused upon the breath, each moment unfolds completely anew, and it is only our own thoughts which colour the world. Each moment is complete nothingness, and also completely everything. Perhaps you have felt this, and know that there is peace to be found every moment, despite the suffering that is all around. All of this is better put into action, and the possibilities are endless: simplifying our own lives is a start. After that, it's easier to do some good for those around us. We can choose to listen without making judgement, acknowledge others' acts of kindness, and know that when people are angry or difficult, it is often because they carry around a lot of hurt and pain and are fearful of being separate, alone or misunderstood. We can empathise because we have experienced this too.

Jason

....

Dear Jason,

Blaming everything on the ego isn't necessarily helping one to learn how to be content. But I do believe it is my ego that caused me to suffer so much in the past. Perhaps I suffered because I thought I was important and should be treated better? If it wasn't for my ego, then I would have walked out on my abusive partners early on. But because I felt compelled to discover why I was not being treated better, I lost sight of those who had the capacity to love me. If I hadn't wanted the gratification of getting someone to love me, then I wouldn't have needed to sacrifice myself, and love would have naturally presented itself. Instead, I clung to my ego and my torment.

Even though I can identify how bullies work, I do not hate them. For if we are all one, then if we hate our neighbour, we're hating ourselves. We are all made of the same stardust, the same

211

chemicals and materials. Like you said, we have experienced feeling hostile in unfair situations, so we can empathise when others do it. When you see violence and hate, you know what it is, because it's inside you too.

My mind was able to receive the trauma visited on me by my perpetrator. And now that I am starting to develop my empathy, I understand the responsibilities that I should have had when I committed a crime. Now that I know that I am in control of my own mind, it would be a travesty to relapse into a blind fog and forget that only I control my future.

Previously I would try to avoid emotional pain, but in reality all I did was attract it. If I had just faced it, I wouldn't have felt half the pain. Isn't that ironic? We must endure pain rather than avoid it, to come out the other side.

To be honest I am terrified still of the unknown and not yet experienced. But by practising meditation I have already seen improvements. I let things settle a bit longer before reacting, which has had benefits already, even if that is just preventing a small dispute. In my meditation I am concentrating on disconnecting from the shell that I occupy, but it can be scary. So I guess my next endeavour is to develop bravery to accept and show compassion to those suffering without being afraid of them.

My very best wishes,
Donna

....

Dear Donna,

Your journey shows how powerful the sense of self can be, even leading us into awful situations. You mentioned how your ego stopped you from walking out on your abusive partners. Those must have been tormenting times, thankfully now past.

You say that what is really needed naturally presents itself, and this reminds me that this is happening all the time. Even in the most dire situations, something is trying to guide us out of the muddle. This is where meditation is useful: when the mind is not thinking of itself, we naturally simplify life, letting go of the habits and relationships which hold us back.

It is good you do not hate bullies, and instead recognise that this feeling of violence and hate can be inside everyone. Do you feel there is room for hatred at all? Perhaps we know this is a reaction that cannot be sustained. You may find this during meditation, when you let thoughts and feelings just be, instead of feeding or burying them.

It is natural to try to reduce pain. But if we can live with our suffering, life is simpler, for everyone. You are right – somehow we can naturally tolerate hard times, and know they will not endure.

Where you find yourself is the perfect place to start developing more empathy towards others. It is clear you are already able to empathise with others, and anything you can do to make life a little more straightforward for everyone is all that is needed. You are probably doing this already: it is clear you are a kind and sensitive person doing her best to understand. This is most inspiring.

Jason

....

Dear Jason,

Your reply got me wondering about hatred. I think people *can* sustain this feeling and work themselves up as a way of dealing with being extremely hurt. It is difficult at times to leave something alone that stirs such strong feelings in us. Maybe this can be used for good things: when you see injustice in the world, if people just let go then nothing would ever improve. But there must be balance, as we spoke of before.

The teachings of meditation frequently complement the therapy I have for my anxiety. I constantly struggle to try hard and get things done, without ever stopping or relaxing. Or I give up entirely because the pressure is too great. But the only solution is to find middle ground. The things I get worked up about can be so insignificant, but it's like a chemical reaction consumes my being with stress until I've found a solution. I'm starting to recognise when I'm doing this, but it's where I draw the line to live a balanced life that is hard. But then after your letter I've been thinking maybe this is about compassion again.

Perhaps if I had more compassion it would take over my self-loathing and life would be more simple. But I fear that a simple life is unproductive. I fear every day that life will be over before I've experienced all it has to offer. I've never met anyone who shares this kind of anxiety, and I don't know where it's come from, but I can tell you: I'm sick of it. I've taken people for granted and not appreciated the small things, like somebody wanting to know me. Someone acknowledging you are a human and knows you are of even a small worth – my God, how lucky. I expected more all the time before prison, always wanting more, never contented. So now I'm trying to practise contentment.

Before, I was extremely generous, because I expected others to behave that way in return. I would beat myself up when they didn't reciprocate, thinking I wasn't generous enough. This is a very warped idea of compassion! I fear how people have manifested their hurt. Some are so narcissistic with their intentions for justice and self-preservation that they are blind to how others feel when they vent their anger, or are blind to how their crimes affected other people's lives. That's me too: I had a skewed idea of how others felt at the time of my crime. I just wanted to be loved but in the process I ruined lives. I rack my brains for how that came to be. It's like the world has been turned upside down and my good intentions have had catastrophic effects. I want to sort that out and understand how it came to be. I want to move on and not repeat past actions. I can't stop analysing how I became a horrible person from trying so hard to be good to everyone except myself. I was always told not to be selfish. Perhaps this isn't good advice for everyone?

Thank you for your deep understanding and accepting I am still human and not a waste to society.

Kindest regards,
Donna

Dear Donna,

It is quite a vision you have for changing injustice in the world. Perhaps this should not be driven by hatred, but instead by a clear view of how the world could be if hatred is reduced. You may have found when the mind calms (even just a bit), beneath all our anxieties there is a glimpse of life unfolding as it should, with no problems or effort.

You are right that there is a balance between being inactive and getting things done. Do you find it helpful to see what is easily achievable? You mention about getting annoyed with small things, and this is where you could easily make a difference. Most people in prison find the routine tedious, and living alongside others is difficult. Just recognising that you are not alone with these feelings is all you need to do. You may need to actively try to remember this throughout the day, but recognising and letting go is all that needs to happen.

I sympathise with your fear that a simple life is unproductive, and you might miss out on what life has to offer. But if we simplify our lives, this allows space for new opportunities. It may not seem like it, but your current time in prison is enormously productive. The insights you are having, and the deepening of your commitment to make positive changes – what more useful way of spending your time? If your mind can settle and recognise the value of simplicity, you will be drawn down new avenues which will be of value to you and everyone else.

The view from our office window seems a little brighter after writing to you.
    Jason

....

Dear Jason,

I thought I was among a diverse mix of people, but the similarities of what has led each of us to committing crime are uncanny. Pain and trauma of different kinds have manifested themselves in

215

a range of impulse acts, resulting in imprisonment. I'm getting clearer on the reason why I'm here: to identify with and have compassion for those I was so terrified of – the angry, violent types. Inside they're hurting, but compassion can't aggravate pain. My fear is decreasing, knowing that it isn't my fault they are angry, but I can empathise with them now, something I couldn't possibly do before. I'm looking deeper than I ever have before, and for once I think I can help people to realise themselves and bring joy to those around me by sharing my recognition of why we make life so hard for ourselves.

I've been reviewing my former friendships, and realise I'd been associating with people who lied to themselves on a daily basis. No wonder I couldn't trust them. Your spring newsletter mentioned how we have to accept who we are at this present moment to achieve our goals of change. This is exactly what has happened. I accept I am not happy with my own company. I can be who I choose to be, without the influence of anyone, so why am I still treating myself as property of somebody else? I'm lying to myself if I think I have to serve others in order to have value.

Being honest with yourself isn't a criticism, it's empowering. A quote from the Buddha says, 'He who calls himself wise is a fool, but he who knows he's a fool, is wise.' I thought I was done at 23, had nothing left to learn. What a fool. If I'm to be an idiot until my old age, what a vast amount of learning and experiences are left for me to discover. That's something to look forward to.

My biggest problem is managing my emotions. Meditation and observation has helped immensely, and your letters too. I have been so moved by the compassion that floods me after realising the simple truths around fear and pain. It can all be battled with compassion, and we are never vulnerable if we understand and have compassion for all. I'm now in a better place.

I have built myself up so far from being on my own, incarcerated; in fact the hardest part will be re-joining society and putting it all into practice. It will be a challenge keeping up my meditation once released, but it helps to have friendly motivation and contact with others of similar interests. Before I was so closely guarded, I kept my personal traumas private. Now I have a habit of speaking more freely with less fear of being laughed at. Kind association with so many helpful guides along the way has enabled this for me. Trying to hide the fact that I was human was a huge contribution to me committing crime. Nobody can keep that up all their life without breaking.

I am very nervous about being released: I'm going into another unknown. I've accepted my fear about it and have let the emotion pour out, so that I can reach a further form of acceptance and strength. I wonder if positive change always needs trauma in order to succeed to the next level. Right now it feels like that!

I sometimes cry so much at how I could possibly have not discovered all this truth just that little bit earlier, and could have had such a fantastic life full of great prospects. Now I'm very restricted and I've caused so much pain, all because I just didn't realise my life was false. I wish I could rewind my life and start over, I wish it with all my might! This will be the hardest thing to let go of.

At least now I have that clarity; some things are even back to front. For example, I used to smoke for clear-headed concentration, yet when I am seeking that now, smoking feels like a distraction, and it even interferes with my meditation. The answers take longer to appear when I've had a cigarette. This is taking the enjoyment out of smoking and it feels dirty. My mind is telling me what it needs at last!

I hope my discoveries, owed to you, will make your day a little better.

Best wishes,
Donna

....

Dear Donna,

It is wonderful you have discovered ways to empathise and understand people you would normally keep away from. You are simply with people who need compassion, empathy and patience. You will come away from all this with a huge understanding of how people work, and it is clear you have discovered something more that can transform every situation you find yourself in.

You mentioned old friendships with people who lie to themselves. I am sure you will find people who are more transparent and open. Perhaps everyone wishes to be like this, but is just afraid to show themselves. Your openness and understanding will put them at ease. The qualities you mention, like openness, honesty and simplicity, are actually here all the time, and arise quite naturally when our thoughts begin to settle. But life is still complex, and making life simpler for everyone is so worthwhile.

Your release is not far away, and this must be an anxious time. I would be pleased to stay in touch when you are released. You may find the following passage helpful for the time ahead. It is by Victor Frankl, a psychiatrist who spent many years in a concentration camp:

> Don't aim at success – the more you aim at it and make it a target, the more you are going to miss it. For success, like happiness, cannot be pursued; it must ensue, and it only does so as the unintended side-effect of one's personal dedication to a cause greater than oneself. Happiness must happen, and the same holds for success: you have to let it happen by not caring about it. I want you to listen to what your conscience commands you to do and go on to carry it out to the best of your knowledge. Then you will live to see that in the long run – in the long run, I say – success will follow you precisely because you had forgotten to think of it.

I understand your wish that you had discovered all this earlier. But don't forget you have many years ahead of you. Something tells me your life cannot fail to be meaningful and fulfilling. Your life up to this point has already uncovered so much.

Thank you for being you,
  Jason

Dear Jason,

I attended the Buddhist group on Thursday, with a bad cold. Those who I thought of as cold and self-centred surprised me. I have never experienced kindness like it! One, almost a total stranger, brought me a coffee, and another plucked herbs from the garden to soothe my symptoms. How can my path have changed so dramatically? Before, when I lived a life of zero compassion, nobody would ever care if I were suffering. Yet, even though I feel I have done little to encourage this, I am overwhelmed by a sense of family and support.

Compassion can really dictate the path of one's life. I think about the lack of it, and its abundance. Compassion can lead people to pursue or give up. If we experience compassion, we may be influenced to right our own wrongs, but without the initial act of compassion, however small, we may be lost forever. Kind actions are exceptionally valuable, no matter how small, when put into this context. I think about the lack of compassion in my family, the way nobody stops the wheel of temporary satisfaction.

My imprisonment is, in some sense, an act of compassion. Had I not met the Prison Phoenix Trust, for example, would I be having these waves of compassion? Prison, at least, has taught me compassion. Where I once regarded it as unnecessary, I now value it above all. If I continue to allow compassion to flow through my life, will I experience more in return? Although I've never experienced it before prison, it has spurred me on to keep on the right path.

Before, doing things to earn adoration and attention never made me happy. There was no compassion in this. If I had put my mind to selfless, absorbing activities that genuinely teach me about life, then I would be where I am now – happy with discovering a direction. Sometimes, perhaps, we have to take other people out of the equation to be able to place ourselves among them.

People are so important to have around. In fact I think they are a life requirement. I used to think I would be safe if I kept to myself. Now the opposite is true. Without people, I wouldn't have gained my inspiration. I hope to help people on their own journeys in the future.

Warmest wishes,
   Donna

....

Dear Donna,

You mention about the importance of experiencing an initial act of compassion. This is all good preparation for when you are released, and your empathy with others will influence the people you meet. You are on quite an adventure, Donna, and with your perception and empathy there will be positive times ahead. Thank you for letting us walk some of the way with you.

   Jason

....

Dear Jason,

I am now out of prison, facing many challenges in my probation period. I have caught up with the essentials, and am trying to find spiritual groups to further my positive new start. I am looking to put a business idea into practice soon, but ideally I'd like to draw on my experiences to help people. I know this will be more difficult but I still want to do it.

It has been stressful coming out of prison and not knowing how to fill my time without being told what to do. I sometimes feel like a freak because this is another world, away from what I had gotten used to. It's hard to talk about prison now, as it's not the norm, and there's only officials with whom I can really discuss it. Writing will be a real outlet. I have made time to meditate when it gets on top of me, but I confess it wasn't my first priority! First I had to rush around to find a direction, something that made me feel of some worth, having something to do. I feel lost without routine and jobs to do. I wonder if I am alone in this.

May you be blessed with peace in all areas of your life.

Yours sincerely,
Miss Donna

....

Dear Donna,

It must be hard adapting to a new life without being told how to fill your time. But you now have freedom to make choices and start to direct your life in the way you wish. The opportunity to start afresh is a gift, and for someone like you who has discovered so much already, the way forward could be a special time.

It is completely understandable that meditation was not top of the list upon leaving prison, and finding a sense of direction was the priority. Now this is starting to take form, ten minutes (or longer if you can manage it) sitting in silence will allow the mind to settle, and new ideas to grow. Getting your bearings can take some time, and a settled mind will enable this to happen unhindered.

Perhaps there is a park nearby you can visit? All around, there are changes which happen quite selflessly, adapting in the most appropriate way to nature. Leaves changing colour in the sunshine, shadows moving, birds going about their business. It is only humans that think and analyse so much – so any break from this is time well spent, and can allow some wonderful discoveries to emerge.

Jason

....

Dear Jason,

I'm looking to move closer to family and repair some of the angst and confusion going on there, because I have kept my confusion over our family break-up bottled up for over a decade. I would have thought, being grown-ups, my parents would have been the ones to initiate explanations of how they feel about our awkward situation, but I'm still waiting, so many years on! I need to break the cycle and confront them with the truth that I really can't handle losing all that we had and not even knowing why.

On a lighter note, I visited a Buddhist temple recently where I lay on the grass in absolute silence and tried to heal the chaos inside me for just an hour. All I could hear was the odd chirp from the birds or an aeroplane. I felt like a kid again – carefree and at one with the delights that summer brings. I remember lying in the park when I was a kid and making shapes of the clouds. I really miss my childhood, sometimes painfully so.

I was ready to find this temple. I was nervous going in, but was greeted with friendly faces. I asked to see the shrine room, and was led into a fragrant room with golden statues – absolutely beautiful. I wasn't sure what to do here, but I wanted to sit quietly, which is what I did! A nun came and chanted for me and then we had a little chat. I felt so humble that I had been accepted without ever having been to a single temple before! I would like to visit again. I found I was abnormally unaware of time. I was just there in the moment. I got a heavy feeling in the shrine room – like a lot of things happen there – a place of realisation and awareness. I wasn't worried about my usual day-to-day anxieties.

I am grateful for your advice on noticing changes happening around in the open air all the time – I kept this in mind whilst I sat on the grass. I watch the birds in the hostel's garden, they fascinate me how observant they are of us! Their eyes are always peering at us to see if we are offering to them or a danger. It makes me laugh a little bit. You are so right that we need to shut off our analytical brains now and then to be able to think of new ideas. I feel great after these moments.

I'm starting a course to learn how to be self-employed tomorrow – another stroke of luck. Perhaps with my refreshed brain something I hadn't thought of will become a great idea! I don't have a plan yet with how I could help others from my experiences. I think I am still learning and it wouldn't be right to help others before I have come full circle and know what I'm talking about. No good in the blind leading the blind! But one day I hope I can put it into a piece of writing or start a mentoring or a life-coaching group aimed at people who had the same issues as me before I went to prison. If I had someone who had acknowledged the pain and anxiety I was feeling at that time, I wouldn't have gone to prison because I wouldn't have given up on myself as I did.

I wish you the best in all that you're doing.

Thank you, for being there,
   Donna

....

Dear Donna,

It must be so difficult having your family break-up, but courageous of you to confront your parents with the wish to sort things out. Perhaps this will be the right time to come together again. This force attempting to bring things together is immensely strong, and it can take so much energy to remain isolated. This is nearly always born out of fear, and it cannot be sustained forever. You may know that one translation of yoga is 'to yoke' or 'join together'.

You mentioned using your experience to help others, and how you would not have gone to prison if you had known someone who acknowledged the pain and anxiety you were feeling at the time. How important it is to know people who allow our feelings to arise and recede. You will be such a marvellous friend to many people, Donna.

Keep well,
  Jason

....

Erwin James

Erwin is Editor in Chief of Inside Time. *While serving 20 years for a life sentence, he went to yoga classes at HMP Nottingham. He also took every opportunity to educate himself while inside, and developed skills as a journalist. From prison he wrote a regular column for* The Guardian *newspaper, called* A Life Inside. *In this story, from his book of the same name, Sid and the attacked prison officer show that, ultimately, outer appearances, roles and how you talk don't really matter, something that meditation helps you to see more clearly.*

Last week, at the reception hatch, I found myself standing behind a fellow prisoner who normally professed to be hostile to 'the system'. I'd often heard him ranting on the landings about one grievance or another. As I approached and saw the man, I expected there to be some kind of argument in progress. Instead, I discovered pleasantries being exchanged.

A parcel had arrived for the man and he was pleading for it to be issued to him early. (He didn't want to wait until the official time on Saturday morning and queue up with everyone else.) 'Please, guv, please – just this once,' he entreated. Eventually, the officer relented. 'Go on then, you scrote,' he said, by now grinning broadly, 'but don't broadcast it, or they'll all be down here grovelling.' The man gushed his thanks, picked up his parcel and scuttled away victoriously.

'Next,' said the officer, before turning to respond to a remark from his colleague in the back. 'I know,' he said, 'they're only nice to your face when they want something.'

As I walked back to my wing, I reflected on the comment. What he said was true, up to a point. Despite being under almost constant observation, people in prison rarely get a chance to show their true colours. Prisoners who appear angry and bitter can be difficult to deal with sometimes – but how much does that really say about their characters? Others may appear to be polite and cooperative, but is that genuine? In jail, ulterior motives abound. Honesty is an elusive quality. But just occasionally something happens which reveals the unambiguous truth about a man's character.

Take Sid, for example, an old acquaintance of mine in the high-security prison system. Sid was as good as any advert for the anti-authority con. His bitterness was compounded as he had just finished a nine-year sentence and was planning to give up a life of crime when he was offered 'one last job' by former cronies. The job turned out to be a set-up, a 'ready-eye', and Sid received an 11-year sentence. As a consequence, his frustrations were acute and prison officers took the brunt. 'I wouldn't piss on one of them if they were on fire,' he told me and others many times – a sentiment which turned out to be deeply ironic.

One day there was a fire in the prison hospital where Sid worked as a cleaner. The smoke was so thick that evacuation had been unruly and frantic. Stranded and alone, Sid stumbled blindly down a stairwell where he came across an unconscious prison officer. Without hesitation, Sid grabbed hold of the man and dragged him to safety – an act which proved that whatever he said on the landings, when it came to the crunch, Sid's humanity was still intact.

By contrast a few days ago, a prison officer followed a prisoner he suspected of drug dealing back to his cell from the visits hall. As soon as the man closed his cell door, the officer took a discreet peep through the spyhole. Sure enough the man was retrieving a concealed package. 'I'll have that!' he yelled triumphantly. But the dealer was quick too. He jumped on the officer and snatched the package back. They fell out on to the landing just as Peanut was walking by. The dealer had the officer in an arm lock.

'Press the alarm bell,' the officer told Peanut. But Peanut – Mr 'Yes guv, no guv, I've changed guv, help me get parole guv' – hesitated.

'That's a direct order!' shouted the struggling officer.

But Peanut's allegiance to the 'criminal code' was greater than his concern for the officer. Instead of pressing the bell, he just turned and walked away.

'You'll regret that!' the officer called after him. Moments later, reinforcements arrived anyway and nobody came to serious harm – no thanks to Peanut.

Afterwards, everybody expected the officer to make Peanut's life a misery. In fact, he chose not to bear a grudge. The next day he called Peanut to the office. 'There will be no recriminations,' he said. 'I understand the dilemma you faced, and the fear of being seen by your peers to be siding with the screws.' Just to show there really were no hard feelings, the officer even offered Peanut his hand – and the nervous prisoner shook it.

It was a magnanimous gesture, and it just goes to show that when it comes to revealing true colours in prison neither side is predictable.

John

OCTOBER 2011

I'm currently serving three years for burglary. And this is not my first time in jail. Since being in here I've been speaking with the Buddhist minister every week and practising meditation daily. I find it amazing how half an hour doing nothing is having such a profound effect on my mood and my life. I really want to change my lifestyle, my drug-taking and my jail time. So often I've just done my time, got out and carried on as before and wonder why the wheels keep falling off and I come back. It's because I don't do anything about it. This time I'm trying hard. I'm going to do the 12 steps and hopefully get to the bottom of my drug addiction. At the moment that's the only option open to me.

NOVEMBER 2011

Just knowing my shortcomings is eye-opening; dealing with them, challenging; overcoming them, utterly amazing.

I'm used to being in a really negative frame of mind, lying, stealing, being deceitful – to name a few. But now, I'm always either positive or neutral, mostly positive. Not a lot can get me down any more. I'm finding it easier to tolerate people who would normally make me angry. I tell people who ask to try meditating and see where it gets them. But I pretty much keep myself to myself. If I'm open and honest, I think anyone who is the same will be drawn to me and everyone else won't. I'm quite happy with my own company now and find that if I get involved with too many people who are not on my wavelength (which are many) I get too wrapped up in their negative energy. But if I sit alone and talk with whoever comes and sits with me, I find that those positive conversations greatly outnumber the negative as they, the negative, soon move away.

JANUARY 2012

It's been a crazy few weeks for me, getting transferred to A wing, different jail, then C wing a week later, then G wing finally after another week. I've had some interesting cellmates. The first, Bruno, was such a nice bloke, I spent three days in his company and feel like we will be friends for a long time. Very similar pasts and outlooks on life. Talked nonstop. Debated karma and fate for two days on and off. Came to the conclusion that there are different words for the same thing. Bruno, he's on his own path (Christian), not mine, and I commend him for his insight. I learnt a lot from him and feel encouraged by his wisdom, as everything he said was self-taught, self-realised. Cellmate number two was the opposite: young, cocky, rude. But we still had a laugh and I still like him, but can't see me or him staying in touch.

Being moved around, being banged up with an uncaring cellmate, having a cold and ear infection all had its toll on my practice of meditation and yoga. Oh, and finishing my detox. Thirteen weeks clean yesterday. I'm better now, feeling fine. I'm settled now on a drug-free, 12-step wing run by RAPt where I'll be for at least six months. I feel alive again. Everyone in here is in the same boat and, yes, we attracted a few open honest companions and I am of course friendly with everyone. Being Christmas, normally it's drink, drugs and being miserably smashed. Not this year, my first clean Christmas and New Year for 20 years, and you know what? I'm happy about it. I'm in the right place to get my drug problem addressed, get my head and heart right, to get a chance to find out who I am again, and who I can be. I still miss my family, my loved ones, my friends. But I now know how to deal with it all.

Since detoxing, I found yoga so useful. It works better than any medication the docs could give us. I feel like yoga in jails, specially on detox wings, is so missed, so misunderstood. I'm trying to speak to people who could sort out a yoga class for us here.

LATER THAT MONTH

Maybe my journey will take me to a place where I can help and inspire people. Maybe it has already. Jan, my counsellor, asked me to take our morning meditation but I was dubious as I wasn't sure if they'd be interested. I won't know till I try, will I? So Monday I'm going for it, I'm putting my fears to bed and going for it.

The people on the RAPt, the 12-step programme I'm on, really know their stuff. The steps have been around for 80-odd years and work. I've only been here for a few weeks but take something useful away daily. Some days I take so much in I find it hard to remember it all. Sharing your experiences with other addicts really helps. I thought NA and AA[2] meetings were pure bullshit and I had all the things I needed to recover if I wanted, but they are really powerful, those meetings. Step one is 'admitting we were powerless over our addiction and our lives had become unmanageable'. Pretty simple stuff, but admitting I was powerless took ages to realise. There is so much knowledge, wisdom, love and compassion in those rooms, I could feel it and see it. This community we have in here, doesn't feel like jail. Just a rehab really, and not even that as we are all clean. We all want recovery. We all want to get a better life for ourselves when we are finished here and finished with jail. Maybe not all of us will succeed. I used to go to any length to get money to score and get high, and now I will go to any lengths to get clean and stay clean.

AGAIN, LATER THAT MONTH

I've such a long way to go. Determination, patience, endurance and honesty will go a long way to helping me on my journey. Letting go helps. Constant reminders to be mindful, skilful and patient seem to come along, unexpected, at just the right time.

Another reminder, to be happy and keep recovery light and not so gloomy, came at a real low point for me. I had been feeling impatient and bored with RAPt, and I thought a letter from my girlfriend with cash in it had gone missing. I was getting thoughts of wanting to hurt people who were annoying. What I'd started learning to do was simply let go, but I could not let go for long any more. I was on a really dark road. So I went to the gym to get it out of me. It worked, as I got back to my cell resigned to the loss of her letter and my Christmas present. I'd really let it go, I was reasonably happy again. But I was confused as to why I had felt so annoyed. Then I saw her letter on my bed waiting for me.

---

2   Narcotics Anonymous and Alcoholics Anonymous.

I'm thinking I got it then because I'd let it all go. Yes, I'd have felt happy anyway if it had turned up. But because I was happy *before* finding it waiting, I was properly overjoyed.

MARCH 2012

This week, I've stopped smoking (again), on the advice from Rupert, my Buddhist minister. I made a vow to stop smoking to myself and no-one else, and when the cravings come I remind myself of my solemn binding promise to myself not to smoke, and I don't. Easy really, except that the irritation I feel at times is overwhelming. It burnt me hard the first night when I was woken by people talking on the wing. I got up to pee and bit their heads off, went back to bed seething that they woke me up. Until I realised my ego was put out, not me.

Fag-free for three days now and counting. My meditating is easier, not clouded by nicotine, my health can only benefit, my money will be better spent or saved. The only downfall is my appetite, easily put in check by not keeping food in my cell. One more advantage is not having to keep on asking for smokes (taking what is not given). I'm not constantly kicking myself for smoking or asking for smokes, so I'm not feeling bad for myself.

APRIL 2012

Recently in looking at Step 4 – making a searching, fearless moral inventory of my life – I made a big mistake: I only included the bad and overlooked the positives. Okay, the negatives far outweighed the positives. But there is always a positive in any situation. I got myself in a mini state of negativity for a few days until, for some reason, I realised I have a great deal to be grateful for. From that day on, I have reminded myself to be thankful and grateful. And there is so much! I get small reminders from random sources. I surprise myself when I talk about stuff and remember I'm also grateful for things I've forgotten about or simply didn't realise, and from this I have less space in my day-to-day life for negativity!

JUNE 2012

I've been kinda struggling for a couple of weeks. Doubting myself, being too self-critical. My meditation took a big hit due to a cold and the subsequent ear ache. An injury I received through football has put paid to my yoga and gym. I can't do the few things that make me feel good and happy. I feel flat, uninspired, unmotivated. I've found my swearing has increased and my mindfulness has decreased. My cold has all but gone but the ear ache is still there.

Apart from this I am doing pretty well. I hit a landmark in my recovery: on the 2nd June, I'll be six months clean. I can't remember a time in my 20-odd years of using when I've had six weeks clean, totally, 100 per cent clean. I'm proud of my achievement. I feel grateful for my sobriety, which in part I have you to thank for. So thank you. The job I now have, as you said, being a beacon, so that people can realise what I have already realised, is pretty darned rewarding.

AUGUST 2012

I wrote before that I really wanted to do yoga and meditate when I could not. I don't know how, but I've really learnt from that experience. Not only does it make the times when I've been able to practise yoga and meditation more valuable and more enjoyable, but somehow I've learnt also not to rely solely on these practices.

Things are also looking up for me. I have a funding assessment on the 21st August for rehab and I'm also waiting to find out if I'll be released on tag to the rehab if I get funding. I know it's all out of my hands and in the future, so I can't get too hung up about these things as I have no control over the outcome. I'm being patient and accepting that, whatever happens, all I need to do is stay positive. Thank you for the hope your letters bring me.

A while ago, I let a bit of negativity creep in and it came up and bit me hard, really quickly. Luckily nothing bad happened but I see how easily it could have. I was inches away from a fight, but luckily I was aware of what I was doing. When I calmed down and reflected, it was clear that I got complacent (again) and let negative thoughts run the show. I'm back on track now but I'm so amazed how quickly it can all go wrong. I will be making more of an effort to stay focused and positive and not get complacent again.

Someone asked me the other day about what a higher power is. I struggled for ages to work out what that's all about. I could understand the concept but really couldn't see what mine was. But when I was asked, it all made sense: if I stay positive and focus on happiness, whatever life throws at me, I will stay happy and positive. There will be nothing, however bad, that I cannot handle. I don't know if he made sense of this, but I gave him one piece of advice: just be grateful for whatever you can be grateful for. Even in the things that hurt and you dislike, there is always something to be grateful for. Make a list and make sure you add something every day. It won't be long for him to see that there is more to be grateful for than not. If by the time he needs to identify his higher power in his step work he cannot see what it is, at least he'll be able to see it working in black and white.

It astounds me, when on reflection, just how much I have to be grateful for – some small, some big and a lot huge. I'm even really grateful that I'm in prison, grateful I've found a path that's for me, that's brought me happiness and freedom from addiction and a miserable life. All from coming to jail. Some would say I should be ungrateful for being separated from my loved ones, but that's far from true because if I didn't get this chance to have a look at my life, and not liking what I saw or what I could see happening, I would have only made their lives harder. I guess I'm not the only one to be grateful that I'm inside!

Exercise: Gratitude

The person who dished up your supper, the friend who gave you a tea bag, the officer who took you to your workshop, the starling who visited your windowsill for a while, the smell of fresh laundered clothes, the taste of your own newly cleaned teeth – the world provides many small things that often pass unnoticed. In turn, you act in various ways to support the world – listening to a mate's troubles (even when you don't want to), letting someone in front of you in the queue, putting your waste (rubbish and human) where it should go, turning off the tap to save the earth's gifts.

233

It is useful to remind yourself – and with real evidence! – that all of us are interdependent with other people and the natural world. We cannot exist as the separate 'me island' it sometimes feels like. It helps to remember that other people need us for their existence and well-being too, and to remember that *everything* has the desire to connect.

Taking five minutes before you sleep and reviewing the day is one way to bring these truths home. Never mind what kind of day it was, or if it seemed there wasn't much human kindness out there. There will have been some. Did anyone feed you today? Did the lights come on? Did someone smile at you? (It sounds corny, but there is power in a smile – in *your* smile.) As you replay the day, reflect on the various ways you've been supported since you woke up. Try to list at least three. You can write them down, these three things you are grateful to from the day. As you remember each incident or person, spend at least five long, slow breaths thanking them in your mind.

And then reflect on what you have done for others, trying to list at least three. Again, as you remember each thing you did, spend five long, slow breaths realising that you have extended kindness to the world.

It's impossible not to realise that even if we regard ourselves or others as the meanest people in the world, there is no escape from being filled to the brim with kindness as everything goes on interconnecting: eating, showering, looking, listening, reflecting...

I take inspiration from small, simple things that bring massive consequences. I was looking out of my window, something I do a lot and I was blown away by the beauty of my view. I'm lucky to have a patch of grass outside and the flowers – some may be weeds – were shining in a way that the word 'weeds' doesn't do justice to. The buttercups, daisies and dandelions were simply beautiful. I got a real sense of being at one with the world, a beautiful feeling that didn't last long, but which will stay with me forever. I read that I shouldn't cling to these experiences. I'm not holding on to that moment, but I cannot forget it. I feel as if it will stay with me forever. I've had similar since then and all from nature, watching the sunset or sunrise, the clouds in the sky, the birds who come calling for food. They all give me hope, inspiration and a feeling of being a part of something massive. I'm grateful again!

OCTOBER 2012

I've found the strength to overcome my fears of embarrassment and have been doing yoga outside while on exercise. Just having the grass and earth under my bare feet feels truly liberating. When my breath and mind are focused, nothing around me matters. I see infinite details in all that I look at and the feeling of peace, relaxation and release I get from half an hour's practice is magical and beats any drug I've ever done. I walk away with a spring in my step and a connection to everything and everyone around me. Sometimes, I feel selfish as I think that everyone should be feeling like I do.

From venturing outside, I've had a few people join me, some temporary but one comes day in day out and we practise together; he teaches me tai chi and I teach him yoga. So after all, I'm not totally alone. We've forged a strong friendship.

Recently I've been finding a balance in my life and the way I think. I've found a few problems, like my partner thinking of leaving me from doubting my potential to change. I've had a knock back for funding for rehab on my release and have faced numerous difficult people on the wing.  Instead of blowing my top or running away, I've dealt with these problems head on, calmly and rationally, and have overcome all but the funding issue, which is getting addressed as I write. I remain hopeful and wonder why it's not my time to go home for rehab now. Your phrase, 'No snow flake falls in the wrong place' springs to mind.

My yoga partner says the universe has different plans for me, so I should continue to help people address their drug issues. He says, 'Who knows? By staying in jail a little longer, you may just save a life.'

It may sound like my mind has changed and I think differently. I do, but my old addict mind keeps trying to sabotage me. But now that I'm aware of its lying ways, I can tell it to go away and shut up every time it pokes its head up. Over time this is getting easier and less frequent. But it is still there, lurking in the shadows, waiting for me to slip up or step off the path of recovery and spirituality that I'm now walking.

I think that with the hope I feel, along with constant practice, determination and patience, I shan't ever wander off that path. Well, if I do, I won't be too far away before I notice and get back on it and definitely not as far away as I have been all my life, in my addiction and criminal activities.

The universe, God, or whatever, does move in mysterious ways and you know what? Now that I'm not trying to control the uncontrollable and letting things happen and unfold as they should, I've got a real sense of freedom, contentment, and above all, hope for whatever it has destined for me.

NOVEMBER 2012

I've just returned from a visit with my girlfriend and her son. Previously, I'd now be suffering with post-visit blues. Basically being separated from something, full of desire. But now it's different – I feel exactly the same towards her but I somehow feel like I'm with her always. Connectedness in action! I read something yesterday, that we cannot pick happiness up without sadness; one doesn't arise without the other. It gives me comfort to know this. I understand now, and I hope to come to realise the full meaning in time.

I will be celebrating one year of being clean soon. Three hundred and sixty-five of 'one day at a time'! Life is easier clean. I learn on a daily basis how to live correctly. I'm grateful to have not resorted to using drugs on the many different occasions that have arisen. I realise that there's no growth without pain, and that gets me through all the painful, difficult experiences I've had and will have.

FEBRUARY 2013

Good news today: my funding for rehab was granted! I'm so glad I persevered and didn't give up after the first refusal, as I would have done in my previous life.

While I was inside the madness of crime and addiction, looking out at everyone 'normal' looked mental. But now I'm outside looking in, the madness sure looks unappealing, ugly and disgusting. The paradox of becoming free, by being locked up, amazes and astounds me every time I think about it!

I can now see what I was trying to achieve while filling my body and mind with drugs as synthetically trying to reproduce what I have now. Spirituality. But with drugs it's like filling a basket with water: it will always leak away, in need of filling again. No matter how much or how quickly you fill it, it always leaves you wanting more. But now I'm filling my basket with stuff of substance: mindfulness, dharma, awareness and spirituality. This needs maintaining, but doesn't leak away. I'm sure my basket will continue to be filled with goodness.

MARCH 2013

Although I'm now out of prison, I hope we can still keep in touch. I was released three weeks ago and chose to go straight into rehab. It took the best part of two weeks to feel comfortable. I was really uneasy, on edge, like a fish out of water. The sound of a car alarm that's identical to the general alarm in jail put my teeth on edge and the all-too-familiar fear flooded back. I'm so glad and grateful for this chance of rehab, as that fear is what I relapse on. It's tricky because the things I have to struggle with outside – housing, benefits, work, clothing and feeding myself – are not of any concern if I'm in prison.

But I need to break this pitiless cycle of addiction, criminality and prison. I now have the strength to do so. In my short three weeks, I have really been challenged and made aware of behaviours that were hard to accept. I've faced fears that have been so ingrained in myself that I was oblivious to them. That too seemed like an unclimbable mountain, but now I'm over it, it's no more than a mole hill. This fear has kept me from feeling, and I mean truly feeling. It blocked me from crying, expressing myself fully. It feels so great to now be able to shed a tear in public!

----------- ‿ -----------

The True Person is not anyone in particular; but, like the deep blue colour of the limitless sky,

It is everyone, everywhere, in the world.

Dogen, 13th-century Japanese Zen teacher

----------- ‿ -----------

The things I missed while in jail – the beauty of nature, children laughing, the stars at night and choosing the company I keep – seemed so important then. But what I find most special is the things I did in jail: meditation, yoga and tai chi. The rest are all beautiful, but what counts is what is going on inside. They all bring joy but some come from outside and some within. Another amazing thing is the welcoming generous and loving acceptance I've found in the fellowship and the local Buddhist group I now attend. It was almost overwhelming at first but I'm finding my feet. Being accepted on face value and trusted again is something that will take a while to get used to, but totally welcome.

Recently I actually let go while meditating, and wow! What an experience. Totally liberating and freeing. The same night and next day I was so full of love, it felt like every drop of love in the universe was coursing through every single molecule of my body. Unfortunately, it did not stay with me for long, but now I'm okay with that. I just enjoyed it while it lasted.

I've met a lot of nice people and I seem to be drawn to people who are on my level and who are spiritual people. I'm so glad of this chance of a new beginning, leaving all the dark people and places far behind me. The idea of setting foot in my home town, to face all my using associates and be reminded of where I came from, fills me with dread. In time I'll be strong enough, but for now I'm happy and safe where I am. I feel no need to test myself.

238

OCTOBER 2013

Life is still tinged with difficulties. Some people still haven't accepted I've changed (yet!). My addictive side still tries to find a way in and money is tight. But I've got somewhere permanent to stay now, my relationships are blooming, my son is back in my life after a 12-year absence on my part. I've found that by doing the next right thing, that good things are happening to me, my home, relationships. Gifts are coming that I really need, but haven't asked for. Life is easier now I've got nothing to hide from. I can accept myself and my past. I'm not sure if I love myself yet but I sure don't hate myself any more.

I'm out of jail six months today, my birthday. What I've got in my life today is the best present I could ever dream of. I got peace of mind!

DECEMBER 2013

Since I wrote my last letter, I have been on a couple more retreats which really deepened my meditation practice. The last one has had a massive effect on me that I am still to find out in my own time. I now love myself, I no longer suffer with fear. It's now just there, being fear, being ignored by me and doing it anyway!

I have had to face up to some difficult stuff lately. I'm meeting up with one of my victims next week through Restorative Justice. That's something I'd never have imagined would happen. Yesterday we went through a mock conference, which knocked me sideways, and I'm still feeling a bit off centre. It's weird really: I have to go through the pain of admitting my faults to overcome them. Sounds so simple, but feels so difficult. There is nothing that can keep me from going through with this, especially fear, or the fear of feeling uncomfortable.

I have felt how I imagine I'll feel after I meet my victim. It feels like positivity but with none of the pleasant emotions. Then after a few days things will settle and the real positivity will appear.

I went through a similar thing of having to let my girlfriend go because she couldn't stop using drugs. I knew what I was doing was right but it felt so wrong. On the positive note, I was asked to do an interview for National Prison Radio. I'm doing a talk for Open Road on how meditation and yoga have changed my life. I now work in a Right Livelihood business, alongside fellow Buddhists. I am to have my Mitra[3] ceremony pretty soon.

JANUARY 2014
Since I last wrote, I have been on another retreat. Afterwards, someone noticed that my face opened up during that week, and on reflection my face opening up was the result of my heart and mind opening up and of me letting a lot more of my past go. In treatment it's likened to putting down rocks that we have been carrying around in a rucksack. That week, I just stopped carrying the bloody thing! I may still have a few pebbles in my pocket, but they will go, eventually.

Could you let me know if there is any way of me giving back to the PPT please?

APRIL 2015
I'm now full-time working for a charity I love and believe in, which treats me well, living in a community in London and about to start my sixth fundraising appeal! My life just keeps getting better.

---

3   Mitra – friend of the order.

I make so many new friends; and the ones I already have, our friendships just keep on getting deeper and deeper. It seems like I'm being appreciated and valued on how I am today and not who I was. That feels good, not feeling judged on my past. I've been asked to help out a lot with some of our Buddhist movement projects, the 12-step programme, our camping festivals, and I had my first commission for the wood-carving I recently took up. The feeling of being appreciated and the gratitude I have around this takes my breath away.

We have been delighted to take John up on his offer of giving something back to the PPT. He has given talks at our yoga teacher training events on the challenges of recovery from addiction, prison life and adjusting to life on the outside.

Nick, HMP Liverpool

Dear Ava,

You introduced me to meditation and yoga and sent me CDs and books, all powerful stuff which has helped me no end to cope with my sentence. Well, time was ticking along nicely and daily I was understanding more of the simplicity of achieving a healthy mind and body by doing little bits of gym and looking forward to bang-up every night to do my yoga and meditation. I work as the wing Shelter rep, dealing with housing and debt issues for other prisoners. I like to be of use to others, while building up some good karma in the process.

Then the wing bully (or one of them) who has eight inches and three stone on me decided because of my quiet and gentle persona he could take some of my belongings. I am less than three years into a life sentence for taking the life of someone who tried to bully me so my reaction was fight rather than flight. No biggie, a bit of fisticuffs and, like all bullies, when he realised I would retaliate he's kept his distance. My issue is the disturbing thought process this left me with. At first toward this bully, then with any sort of disagreement, I would catch myself thinking bad intentions, at one point even considering arming myself. Thankfully, I would catch a hold of myself before acting anything out. The thought process was pretty unsettling and I ended up thinking, 'Fuck all that yoga shite. It's alright developing a peaceful caring ethos out there, but in prison where arseholes pounce on any sign of weakness, no. I fear bullies and they sense that fear.' Not realising it's a fear of me losing the plot and ending up with another corpse on my conscience to attack me in my nightmares. I dealt with this by not going to the gym or doing yoga and getting stoned whenever the opportunity arose. I wasn't a happy bunny.

Then last week out of boredom I got my yoga CD out again. And hey, I feel a lot clearer, calmer and better again – better than any spice could make me feel. Already my sleep is coming back, and not drug-induced. And my mental foes from slumberland seem to have run out of fuel. I ain't saying it's an overnight success, but Rome wasn't built in a few shifts. Those thoughts are a lot rarer and being nipped in the bud and my sense of humour is coming back. It also felt good saying no to the spiceman at the weekend. I feel I have to go over old ground to get back to the place I was, but I enjoyed the journey last time so why not again? The simple obvious path to my well-being hasn't left me, but the other way round. I see now it's all building blocks.

We have been on lock-down much of this last week as gang wars rage on some of the wings. This has left me with plenty of time to sit in meditation, which has me feeling quite content internally while complete chaos rages all around.

Peace to you Ava,
Nick

....

Dear Nick,

Thank you for such a great letter; well expressed, honest and thoughtful. It's good news you've found our CD again.

The most impressive thing in your encounter with the bully was the way you watched the process going on in your mind, saw how clearly it can mislead us and your reaction to it. At first, 'f*** it! Things are different inside!' And later, something – boredom you say, who knows? – made you start again. Now you may find that because of the turbulence you went through, your practice will be all the more meaningful and give you the inner ballast to keep the ship on an even keel. You have the will and the fortitude.

Looking forward to hearing from you. Our best wishes and encouragement,
Ava

....

Gratitude

Why is it that after putting in time and effort in meditation, so many people get an overwhelming feeling of gratitude? One woman who writes to the PPT said, 'I never felt grateful for (or even comfortable with) being alive, until I started looking within and talking to myself (not in a mad way) and to what or whoever is out there... I started thanking whatever is out there...that's when I really started to feel free!'

You'll remember John earlier in the book saying that he was actually thankful for going to prison, as it allowed him to find a path out of his addiction and miserable life. Years after his release, Andrew in this section took a pilgrimage back to Swansea to sit and gaze from a distance at the prison, because he'd discovered a peace and spaciousness beyond words while locked up there.

The letters in this section – and in other parts of the book – reflect that when real gratitude wells up, you naturally seem less able to ignore the needs of other people, and are drawn 'to making someone else's life a little more bearable,' as Eric says. Nigel's body is packing up on him, after leading an active, physical life, yet he's deeply grateful for what he *can* do, thanks to meditation and to his yoga teacher. Patrick's life outside of prison is hard, but he's glad for what he's got, and finds himself spontaneously giving to other people.

Andrew said he still doesn't fully understand what happened to him in Swansea. Why, when your conditions seem so bleak, should gratitude come forth? It doesn't make sense...until you spend some time letting go of everything as you focus on your breathing.

Nigel, HMP Winchester

Dear PPT,

I am a 70-year-old man and I've been in prison for the last three-and-a-half years with some more to do. For more than 30 years I was a soldier in a tough Scottish regiment. In most aspects of work we did everything at double time. We ran everywhere and the spirit of competition was encouraged. Everything was treated as a challenge. Now in my twilight years my body has worn down. I have osteoarthritis in both hips and a prolapsed disc.

Due to the unfit and injured body state, I now have to slow down everything I do. I walk with the aid of two sticks, and find it very painful at times. When it was advertised on our wing noticeboard that yoga classes were being held once a week, most of the prisoners laughed, saying it was a girlie thing. When the classes started, most of the inmates went just to spend time outside of their cells. However after a few weeks the numbers dwindled. The novelty wore off and the tough guys actually didn't find it easy and left. There are a number of us that now regularly attend.

The physio in Winchester Hospital had given me exercises to do while in my cell, but these were doing me no good at all. They were keeping my body mobile but they were not pushing me in any way. I felt I was just fading away. I went to my GP here in the prison and asked him if yoga would do me any harm. He said it would be good for me as long as I did not overdo it.

My first session I treated with a little caution. However, the exercises were not difficult but the relaxation and calm exercises (wow) were fantastic. I left that class as though I had no cares in the world. I try and push my body to do more, and find that most of the pain I have is all in the mind. I respect what my body tells me as I'm not a young thing any more, but I refuse to become a cripple. I continue to do my exercises in my cell but find I get a great deal of relief from my relaxation, though I feel that the thought process is just as important as the physical. It's so important to be at peace. Our mentor Judy is a quiet woman whose voice is mellow but insistent. Long may she carry on.

I have now become a person of peace and tranquillity, whereas before I took everything at face value. I now look for the good in people and apply everything I have been taught in yoga classes: peace, calmness and the ability to understand other people's problems. There are always people worse off than myself. Thank goodness for meditation.

My wife of over 30 years has been diagnosed with terminal cancer and COPD. She is in a hospice where she gets comfort from friends and family. Just over a year ago, my youngest daughter (step-daughter) was told she had terminal cancer. However, she is in remission at this present time. Thank God. My yoga and meditation have helped me through this very stressful time and without it then I don't think I could cope.

With thanks to you, and to yoga and meditation,
   Nigel

....

Dear Nigel,

Many thanks for your letter. It's unusual to hear from someone who has experienced such a range of physical and mental fitness. Your time in the Scottish Regiment must have given you resilience and determination. It looks like these qualities will always be with you.

There will always be a number of men who think yoga is just for women, though this number is shrinking every year. It takes discipline and patience, and not everyone is good at this; your time in the army must have given you a lot of fortitude and resilience.

I used to be an engineer, and part of my job involved understanding grades of steel. Some are hard and difficult to cut, but snap like glass under too much stress. Others are malleable and can be curved and worked (like the bodywork of a car) without returning to their original shape. You may know that steel springs are a combination of hardness and flexibility – they possess resilience and can move but still return to their original useful shape again. There is an analogy with yoga here – resilience,

247

strength and flexibility expressed in an unassuming way. None of this is dependent upon age. All that's required is concentration and patience.

You are right that our thoughts and physical well-being are equally important – as the practice progresses they seem inseparable. You may know that one translation of yoga is 'to join' and it is good to know that Judy has been assisting the class to discover this themselves.

I am sorry your wife and daughter are so unwell. It's good your wife has support from her visitors and your daughter's cancer has slowed. You seem to accept these situations peacefully. Just understanding that life can be difficult for everyone makes it easier to relate to other people. Perhaps you have found that your tolerance and acceptance is helping others in prison too.

It is great knowing you, Nigel.

Your friend,
Jason

....

Benjamin Zephaniah

In a BBC national poll, Benjamin was voted the nation's third favourite poet of all time, and the only living one in the top ten. You might have heard him on the radio, or seen him on TV, most recently in Peaky Blinders *as Jeremiah Jesus. This story of Benjamin's reflects what many people serving sentences who have started to meditate come to realise about prison officers: that while they may appear different, there is actually no difference between you.*

I was in a prison called Winson Green, which is now Birmingham prison, and I had a little thing going on with one of the prison officers. He discovered that I like martial arts, and he used to come and do the night shift and he had a little room at the bottom of the corridor, and when everybody else was asleep he used to come and let me out. I don't know how technically allowed that was, but we'd move his desk to one side of his room and then we would spar and spar and spar, karate style. And at the end of it we used to sit down and do a couple of minutes just meditating – deep breathing, we didn't really call it meditation – just like calming down, centring ourselves. Then I'd go back to my cell, and in the morning he'd let me sleep a little extra.

I remember saying to him one day, 'I'm glad you do this with me because it's really good for me,' and he said, 'It's good for me too.' So actually, if more prison staff practised yoga, and we had prisoners practising yoga – come on: it just makes for a more harmonious environment. People will understand people a lot better. They'll respect each other more. It is genuinely a win–win situation.

Like everyone, prison officers have stresses and strains in the job. We kind of think that prison officers – when I was a kid, we used to call them screws – are all the same. But that's like them thinking that all prisoners are the same. They have their own internal politics, they don't all get on with each other. There are different tribes within their community. And most of them – regardless of what we say about people in uniform – they're not all there because they're on a power trip. They genuinely, genuinely want to try and do good and help people. I can see them trying to reach out sometimes and not feeling that they're going to get that from the prisoners, it's not a touchy feely situation. And I can understand why they're going to feel frustrated. Because it doesn't matter how you cut it, they have a uniform on. And the prisoners, if they have a uniform, it's the uniform of prison. There's very few things that bring them together. There's very few things that they can relate to together, maybe. But if they're practising, like me and this guy who were practising martial arts together, doing a little bit of deep breathing together, it's the one thing we could do together. And as he said, it helped him just as much as it helped me.

Eric, HMP Leyhill

In February I helped deliver a workshop on the experience of older prisoners at a 'Quakers in Criminal Justice' conference. I came away feeling that I'd received a great deal more than I had given. Haven't done any public speaking for many a long year but found that, much like riding a bicycle, once I got started I felt quite at ease.

I say thank you every day for the blessings in my life, of which there are many. Whatever serenity lies at the centre of my being flows from accepting ownership of everything I have done in life, not least of the hurt and sadness I have caused other people. That acceptance is rooted in the knowledge that there is a purpose in everything that happens.

When psychologists tell me they think I am being stoical, some say philosophical, about the length of time I have been in prison and I reply that I believe I am in exactly the right place, at the right time, to learn things I need to know, they look at me rather quizzically. I find it difficult to explain to them that there are things I have come to 'know' since I began sitting in meditation. I can't always put into words what it is that I 'know' or how I came to know these things. Neither would I suggest that what it is that I 'know' is of any particular use to another. But I am sure that it is right for me.

If one believes, as I do, that life has a purpose, a meaning, then it follows that there is something beyond what we know as life. What I have come to accept is that life is but a preparation – albeit an oft-repeated preparation – for something else. What this something else is I do not know, and would not even want to hazard a guess, and I might even be wrong: perhaps there is no purpose.

It doesn't really matter either way. What matters is that we follow the leadings of the heart and not the head, and seek to be as kindly and loving as possible to all things, animate and inanimate, during our lives. If doing this achieves nothing other than making someone else's life a little more bearable then that surely is worth the effort, isn't it? If, on the other hand, there is a purpose to life then at least we will have done something towards gaining a better understanding of our true nature.

Patrick

Dear Rachel,

In my heart, I know there is no place in heaven for bad people and some forms of Christianity seem very strict indeed. It scares me very much at the moment because I try to do good deeds and be a good person but my past stays with me. All I've ever done is prison and care homes. I find it very useful to talk to you Rachel.

Patrick

....

Dear Patrick,

I'm sorry you're afraid of going to hell. You've said this before so I hope it's okay if I tell you what I think about that. Basically, I don't think heaven is full of good people who've never done the things you have. It sounds like it's full of people who've asked for and received forgiveness, and changed their ways. Jesus himself shows that. Like when he said to one of the guys crucified next to him, 'Tonight you'll be with me in heaven.' He didn't ask the man what he'd done to get crucified – the guy might have been a murderer as well as a thief, but because he was sorry and asked Jesus to remember him when he came to his kingdom, Jesus invited him in.

I read a book by a Catholic priest and his brother and sister-in-law all about this. They were talking about that bit in Matthew's gospel (chapter 25, v.31-46) where Jesus says people will be divided into sheep (going to heaven) and goats (going to hell) depending on what they've done. The priest asked the nuns they were talking to, 'How many of you have ever done anything wrong, walked by on the other side of the road when someone was in need?' All the nuns put up their hands. 'Uh oh. You're all goats! But wait a second – how many of you have ever helped someone in need, in any way?' Everyone put up their hands again. 'Hey, you're okay after all. Jesus said that anyone who did that would be welcomed into heaven!'

See, all of us do good *and* bad things; what matters is that you *try* to do good, like you told me you do, Patrick. It's the people who don't admit they've done wrong, or don't care, that have real problems. You keep trying and you'll be okay. Every day, sometimes every hour or even more often, we have the chance to make someone's life a bit nicer or a bit more difficult – isn't that amazing? All you have to focus on is *today, right now.*

Let me know how you're getting on, and what good things you've enjoyed doing to make the world brighter!

With love,
  Rachel

....

Patrick replied with news of his accommodation, and work. He also said he was giving part of his income to an overseas charity, and that he'd given money to a beggar one day, and immediately afterwards, he'd come into some good luck. He was full of joy. Rachel's reply was helpful:

Dear Patrick,

I think you'll always be able to find joy in life if you help others however you are able, even though you're unlikely to always get an immediate reward afterwards!

You mentioned that some days you lose your faith or don't feel like reading your Bible. That's normal. It's like some days you may not feel like talking to your friends, even though you get on well with them. But you'll still be a good friend to them as long as

253

you don't neglect them for ages, or refuse to help them out when they need you. I reckon God wants us always to be enjoying the present moment and choosing the way to be in all the little things we do, so we make the world a more enjoyable place for people around us, not worse. If you're doing that, being patient even if someone at KFC is a bit rude, say, then you're close to God even if you don't feel like it.

Reading the Bible, going to church, doing yoga and meditation, praying, etc., are ways that we can keep reminding ourselves of what's really important in life, which is doing like Jesus said: 'Love the Lord your God with all your heart, all your soul, and all your mind and your neighbour as yourself.' If you're doing that, you're okay.

You're doing great – three months out of jail and living well! Everyone's rejoicing! Keep it up, Patrick.

All the best from all at the PPT,
Rachel

....

Andrew

Unlike most of the other accounts in this book, which are from letters, we had asked Andrew to write something for our quarterly newsletter a few years ago, after he'd been released from prison.

When I arrived at Reception on a cold January evening I was still traumatised. The process of arrest, bail and Crown Court sentencing had left me drained. By the time I reached my cell, I didn't care what happened to me.

In the first few days I was stripped of all the things that had formed a part of my life outside. My situation was only temporary, but at that moment in time I was deprived of family, friends, home, job and all those possessions that had become ridiculously important over the last 20 years. The cell door just referred to me as 5346. I didn't know who I was any more. As the days rolled into weeks, something else within me began to collapse and die – thought form. You see, I had also derived my sense of self from my mental positions and opinions. I had conditioned myself to believe that I was my thoughts. I had always had strong views on political issues and sometimes reacted violently to events that did not reflect my own egoistic values. These dense mental positions had put me in prison in the first place, because my original offence was connected with heavy protests against the war in Iraq. In my prison cell the mental image of who I thought I was died.

Through meditation I began to see the folly of the common human condition, of identifying with a false sense of self. I began to notice how many of us derive our sense of self from the clothes we wear, from the food we eat, or even the car we drive! The person who I thought I was just didn't work any more. All these years I had been identifying with an illusion.

Meditation is not easy in a prison cell. It is almost impossible to sit still in comfort. It is restless and noisy with an undercurrent of negative energy. Nevertheless, it was through the practice of meditation that I began to become aware of something within myself that I had never felt before. It manifested itself as an inner presence – a deep peace that seemed to form a central core to my existence. For the first time in my life I began to experience the essence of who I was.

I still do not fully understand what happened to me in HMP Swansea. It may not be possible to use thought to understand that which is beyond thought. Maybe the phenomenon was familiar to St Paul when he used the expression 'the peace which passeth all understanding'. Here I was locked up in a small room, and in the face of my suffering I felt peace.

The chapel was the quietest place in prison and I used to attend every Sunday. Although I am not a Christian, the service became important to me. There is a strong energy in any place of worship and you can tap into that energy irrespective of your ideology. When we all sang the hymns together it was undoubtedly a spiritual experience. Prior to my transformation I would have rejected and ridiculed it. For many years I had labelled myself an atheist, but now there was no longer a need for labels. I knew who I was! When we strolled back to D wing afterwards, I had a deep knowing that my heavy mind structure had gone forever.

My original strategy for dealing with my situation, developed during the early days of incarceration, was to look after number one, keep myself to myself and to hell with everybody else! The strategy is based on the illusion that you are separate from the rest of humanity. This strategy failed me within a couple of weeks. The one that followed took a very different line. Because I had started practising metta meditation on the top bunk, the new strategy took on the characteristics of offering loving kindness to all people. The happiness and well-being of all inmates, officers and staff became my prime preoccupation in prison.

Through compassion, understanding and love I started to support the young men on D wing. This was a new experience to me, a selfish person. When my egotistical self fell apart I could see a new and sacred truth: my own happiness could only be found through others.

When I was no longer identified with forms I became free from a mental imprisonment. There was suddenly a space around my prison life, around the emotional highs and lows, even around the pain itself. Above all, there was a space between thoughts.

It doesn't really matter what you call this experience, it's beyond words. It came to me because I was in a situation of intense suffering. Humans often experience transformation when faced with deep suffering – the death of a loved one, a serious illness, prison, physical pain.

I returned to Swansea in January 2007 for a weekend 'pilgrimage', staying in a guest house 200 yards from the prison.

The view of the sea and Oystermouth Bay was similar to the one from my cell two years earlier. I spent many hours sitting on a bank opposite the prison contemplating my 'old home' and all the men residing there. Despite the grey stone walls and silver rolls of barbed wire snaking along the parapets, it remains my cathedral, the most sacred place on earth.

Exercise: Loving Kindness

Most people who find their lives changing through meditation say it's important to just have one main practice to do; people in prison have told us that the method described in Part I of this book helps them find real peace inside, and that's of course what we're recommending. Sticking to one practice keeps you from becoming a 'spiritual magpie' who hops from one thing to the next when the first thing gets difficult. Choosing to stick with something over a long period can bring great lessons and deepen your appreciation of it, and of yourself.

Even as you stick to your main practice, there are other ways of training the mind that can support you on your way. One of these is loving kindness meditation or *metta bhavana*, which Andrew and others mention. *Metta* means kindness or loving kindness, and *bhavana* means development. This meditation helps shift your fundamental stance towards life, the world and everything and everyone in it – including yourself – to one of kindness. This might seem like a massive leap if life hasn't treated you kindly: why does the world deserve my love and kindness? But this activity can flip things on their head: it empowers you to cultivate an inner quality that you may see lacking in the world, and in so doing, provide it for yourself and for the world.

Here's how you do it:

1. Sit in one of the meditation postures described in Part I. Take a minute to focus on your breath and to be aware of your body, sitting here.

2. After a minute, begin to wish yourself well. With each in-breath and each out-breath, see yourself sitting here, in your mind's eye, and say on the out-breath,

   May I be safe and well.

On the next out-breath, say to yourself,

May I be free from suffering.

And on the third out-breath,

May I live with joy and ease.

Keep doing this for two or three minutes. Don't worry if it just seems like you are saying the words, without much feeling of kindness towards yourself behind them. That will come.

3. Now bring to mind someone who you like, or respect, for whom it is easy to generate good feelings. And wish that person well. On the first out-breath,

May you be safe and well.

And on the next out-breath,

May you be free from suffering.

And on the third out-breath,

May you live with joy and ease.

Do this for two or three minutes.

4. Next, bring to mind someone neutral, who doesn't stir up strong feelings one way or another, someone you don't have much to do with but whose path you cross from time to time. For two or three minutes, wish them well, using the out-breath and the words, as above.

5. Now bring to mind someone you find difficult, with whom there's a little friction. Don't start with your number one enemy, if you have one, or someone who has made your life really miserable – that can be overwhelming, though maybe in time, you find you can wish them well too. Start with someone a little

easier. And wish them well using your out-breath and the words of kindness.

6. Finally, with each out-breath, extend your good will and kindness to the whole prison and everyone who lives and works there, to the area outside the prison, the whole of the country, the whole world and all its human and non-human creatures, and finally to the whole universe. You can say, *May all creatures be safe and well* and so on.

A Last Word

Well, here we are, at the end of the book. But it's not the end of opportunities to look inside, for me or for you.

In each of us, there is a process of growth and change, a pull towards wholeness and healing. Whether you nurture it or not, this runs through the length of your life, patiently waiting for you to pay it some attention.

Silent meditation helps your process and my process and everyone else's flourish, the way rain can turn a dry, brown countryside green. With time and practice, you see that letting go into the peace inside, giving over to the simplicity and silence of the breath, and giving up trying to control everything helps this process along. At times, even when life gets really challenging, you may sense that nothing at all is missing or out of place. Instead, you may find yourself simply being with what is, without telling yourself (and other people) lots of stories about what is happening. This can be a place of not only peace, but also joy, freedom and creativity. And of love.

This lifelong process is also helped along by friendship. Know that the letter writers at the PPT are happy to exchange letters with you for as long as you like. We don't claim to have any answers – you'll only find those inside yourself – but we will gladly walk together with you on this strange, difficult, beautiful path. Tramp, tramp!

Some Prison Terms Explained

These terms from the letters may need explanation if you aren't familiar with prison culture:

Basic The lowest regime level for a prisoner, below 'standard' and 'enhanced'. These levels form the basis of the prison system's Incentives and Earned Privileges (IEP) schemes in England and Wales, designed to encourage good behaviour. On basic, there is less contact with other prisoners and the outside world and no television.

Block Also known as the seg, the segregation unit, a unit within the establishment that contains prisoners who are segregated from the normal population. This segregation may be because of disciplinary punishment or for the prisoner's own protection.

Cat D/D Cat In England and Wales, category D is the category in which those adult male prisoners who pose the lowest risk in relation to security and protection of the public are placed. Cat D prisoners are ideally placed in open prisons (or D cats) to ease their transition back to normal life. At the other end of security are high security or Cat A prisons, for those prisoners who, if they escaped, are deemed to be dangerous to the public. In between are Cat C and Cat B. The security categories for women and young offenders in England and Wales, and for prisons and prisoners in Scotland, Northern Ireland and Ireland, are each unique. Over the course of one's sentence, it is normal to move down in category towards D before release.

IEP Incentives and Earned Privileges: see 'Basic'.

Inside Time The national monthly newspaper for prisoners, with an estimated readership of 50,000. It is distributed to every prison and special hospital in Britain.

Listener The Listener scheme is a peer support service which aims to reduce suicide and self-harm in prisons. Samaritans volunteers select, train and support prisoners to become Listeners. Listeners provide confidential emotional support to their fellow inmates who are struggling to cope.

On the out Outside of prison; in life before or after one's time in prison.

PIPE Psychologically Informed Planned Environments are specifically designed environments where staff have additional training to develop an increased psychological understanding of their work. This enables them to create a supportive environment which can facilitate the development of those living there. PIPEs are not treatment programmes themselves, but are environments or cultures which enable offenders to maintain developments they have previously achieved. PIPEs are progression units for people who have completed 'high-intensity treatment'.

RAPt The Rehabilitation for Addicted Prisoners Trust, a UK charity delivering drug and alcohol services – in prisons and in the community – which help people move away from addiction and crime.

Script Short for 'prescription', usually referring to a methadone prescription.

About the Prison Phoenix Trust

The Prison Phoenix Trust (PPT) supports UK and Irish prisoners in their spiritual lives through meditation, yoga, silence and the breath. We work with people of all faiths and those with none, and recommend breath-focused stretches and meditation sensitively tailored to students' needs. This safe practice offers students the possibility of ultimate peace of mind. The PPT encourages prisoners – and prison staff too – through correspondence, books, CDs, newsletters, radio programmes, free taster workshops and weekly classes.

A woman named Ann Wetherall started the charity. She'd been working in 1986 with the Religious Experience Research Centre, gathering and archiving accounts of people's religious experiences. Ann and others wondered if people in prison might have more of these experiences than people in general.

After putting articles in prison newspapers and literature, the Centre started hearing from prisoners. Many said they had never told anyone about their mystical or religious experiences, because they worried people might think they were mad.

Deeply moved by the responses, Ann wanted to stay in touch with the prisoners who had written, learn from them, and do something – she wasn't quite sure what – to help spirituality in prison flourish. This was beyond the remit of the centre she was working with, so Ann set off on her own.

As she continued to write and meet with prisoners she developed a vision of people in prison using their cells as places of spiritual growth. Soon she was speaking of the parallels of prisoners with monks and nuns, whose rooms are often called cells. For several years, Ann and a group of friends wrote letters to prisoners from a room in her home, encouraging them in their meditation and spiritual journeys. They called the organisation the Prison Ashram Project. In 1988, they registered as a charity, changing the name to the Prison Phoenix Trust. They were still working from Ann's home, but now with a form that would allow the Trust to grow.

Almost three decades later, the Prison Phoenix Trust is in touch with more than 5700 prisoners annually, sends out over 10,000 newsletters each quarter, supports over 140 weekly yoga and meditation classes, and works in prisons in England, Wales, Northern Ireland, Scotland and Ireland. To each of the 2500 letters from prisoners who request help each year in starting a practice in their cell, we respond with a personal letter, one of four resource books or two CDs we've produced specifically for prisoners, and the offer of continuing support through letters back and forth. We also work with prison officials to set up weekly classes.

There are nine staff (mostly part-time) in a small office in Oxford, committed to the well-being of prisoners and prison staff; volunteer yoga coordinators in Scotland and Ireland/Northern Ireland; a network of over 80 yoga teachers who invariably say their prison classes are their favourite classes out of all that they teach; and a team of volunteers, including those who write to prisoners, dedicated to the charity's mission. The work has grown beyond what Ann may have ever imagined when she died in 1992. But her vision of prison cells as places of spiritual growth remains at the heart of the Trust.

Sam Settle is a yoga teacher and meditator. In his twenties he spent five years at Suan Mokkh monastery in Thailand, where he was ordained as a monk. He has taught weekly yoga and meditation classes at Aylesbury and Feltham Young Offender Institutions and at HMPs Grendon and Bullingdon and leads workshops in prisons across the UK and Ireland. Sam has worked for the PPT since 2003, and became its Director in 2010.

All royalties from the sale of this book go directly to support the charitable activities of the Prison Phoenix Trust, including sending this book at no charge to people in prison who request it.

Acknowledgements

The most important people in the making of this book have been those behind bars who meditate. Only a small sample appear here, but the determination of each one inspires me when I read letters from inside, or talk to people who practise meditation and yoga in prison. I'm also grateful for the insight and friendship found in letters going the other way too, from staff and volunteers: thank you to all who write, whether or not your letters appear in this volume.

I feel fortunate to have met Polly, the artist, and to have worked so easily with her. I am grateful for Sylvia Ostertag's poems, and to Wendy and Sue for having translated them from German.

The PPT crew took up slack in the week-to-week running of the charity when I was away, absorbed by this project. Jason and Lucy went the extra mile uncomplainingly with background work on the book and giving constructive criticism at each stage, though it owes a great deal to everyone at the PPT.

I deeply appreciate the honest feedback on the manuscript from my wife Julia and from Jan, Brent, Sandy, Dolores, Aron, Tom, Nicholas and Erwin. Katherine was immensely reassuring when it came to the legalese of the contract. Jessica, Daisy and Vicki at Jessica Kingsley Publishers were patient, clear in their direction and continually encouraging.

Thanks to all of you.